# The Best
# *Men's Stage Monologues*
# of 1999

*Other books by Jocelyn A. Beard*

100 Men's Stage Monologues from the 1980s
100 Women's Stage Monologues from the 1980s
The Best Men's/Women's Stage Monologues of 1990
The Best Men's/Women's Stage Monologues of 1991
The Best Men's/Women's Stage Monologues of 1992
The Best Men's/Women's Stage Monologues of 1993
The Best Men's/Women's Stage Monologues of 1994
The Best Men's/Women's Stage Monologues of 1995
The Best Men's/Women's Stage Monologues of 1996
The Best Men's/Women's Stage Monologues of 1997
The Best Men's/Women's Stage Monologues of 1998
The Best Stage Scenes for Men from the 1980s
The Best Stage Scenes for Women from the 1980s
The Best Stage Scenes of 1992
The Best Stage Scenes of 1993
The Best Stage Scenes of 1994
The Best Stage Scenes of 1995
The Best Stage Scenes of 1996
The Best Stage Scenes of 1997
The Best Stage Scenes of 1998
Monologues from Classic Plays 468 B.C. to 1960 A.D.
Scenes from Classic Plays 468 B.C. to 1970 A.D.
100 Great Monologues from the Renaissance Theatre
100 Great Monologues from the Neo-Classical Theatre
100 Great Monologues from the 19th C. Romantic & Realistic Theatre

**Smith and Kraus** *Books For Actors*
## THE MONOLOGUE SERIES
The Best Men's / Women's Stage Monologues of 1998
The Best Men's / Women's Stage Monologues of 1997
The Best Men's / Women's Stage Monologues of 1996
The Best Men's / Women's Stage Monologues of 1995
The Best Men's / Women's Stage Monologues of 1994
The Best Men's / Women's Stage Monologues of 1993
The Best Men's / Women's Stage Monologues of 1992
The Best Men's / Women's Stage Monologues of 1991
The Best Men's / Women's Stage Monologues of 1990
One Hundred Men's / Women's Stage Monologues from the 1980s
2 Minutes and Under: Character Monologues for Actors
Street Talk: Character Monologues for Actors
Uptown: Character Monologues for Actors
Ice Babies in Oz: Character Monologues for Actors
Monologues from Contemporary Literature: Volume I
Monologues from Classic Plays
100 Great Monologues from the Renaissance Theatre
100 Great Monologues from the Neo-Classical Theatre
100 Great Monologues from the 19th C. Romantic and Realistic Theatre
A Brave and Violent Theatre: 20th C. Irish Monologues, Scenes & Hist. Context
Kiss and Tell: Restoration Monologues, Scenes and Historical Context
The Great Monologues from the Humana Festival
The Great Monologues from the EST Marathon
The Great Monologues from the Women's Project
The Great Monologues from the Mark Taper Forum

## YOUNG ACTOR SERIES
Great Scenes and Monologues for Children
Great Monologues for Young Actors
Multicultural Monologues for Young Actors

## SCENE STUDY SERIES
Scenes From Classic Plays 468 B.C. to 1960 A.D.
The Best Stage Scenes of 1998
The Best Stage Scenes of 1997
The Best Stage Scenes of 1996
The Best Stage Scenes of 1995
The Best Stage Scenes of 1994
The Best Stage Scenes of 1993
The Best Stage Scenes of 1992
The Best Stage Scenes for Men / Women from the 1980s

If you require pre-publication information about upcoming Smith and Kraus books, you may receive our semi-annual catalogue, free of charge, by sending your name and address to *Smith and Kraus Catalogue, 4 Lower Mill Road, North Stratford, NH 03590. Or call us at (800) 895-4331, fax (603) 643-1831.*

# The Best
*Men's Stage Monologues*
**of 1999**

*edited by Jocelyn A. Beard*

**The Monologue Audition Series**

**SK**
A Smith and Kraus Book

Published by Smith and Kraus, Inc.
177 Lyme Road, Hanover, NH 03755

Copyright © 2001 by Smith and Kraus, Inc.
All rights reserved
Manufactured in the United States of America

First Edition: February 2001
10 9 8 7 6 5 4 3 2 1

CAUTION: Professionals and amateurs are hereby warned that the plays represented in this book are subject to a royalty. They are fully protected under the copyright laws of the United States of America, and of all countries covered by the International Copyright Union (including the Dominion of Canada and the rest of the British Commonwealth), and of all countries covered by the Pan-American Copyright Convention and the Universal Copyright Convention, and of all countries with which the United States has reciprocal copyright relations. All rights, including professional, amateur, motion picture, recitation, lecturing, public reading, radio broadcasting, television, video or sound taping, all other forms of mechanical or electronic reproductions such as information storage and retrieval systems and photocopying, and the rights of translation into foreign languages, are strictly reserved. Pages 116–123 constitute an extension of this copyright page.

The Monologue Audition Series  ISSN 1067-134X

**NOTE: These monologues are intended to be used for audition and class study; permission is not required to use the material for those purposes. However, if there is a paid performance of any of the monologues included in this book, please refer to the permissions acknowledgment pages to locate the source who can grant permission for public performance.**

# Contents

*The Adulterer,* Jussi Wahlgren . . . . . . . . . . . . . . . . . . . . . . . . . . . 1
*Bad Buddhists*, Robert Vivian . . . . . . . . . . . . . . . . . . . . . . . . . . . 2
*Blue Food,* Janice Fronczak (3) . . . . . . . . . . . . . . . . . . . . . . . . . 3
*Blue Skies Forever,* Claire Braz-Valentine (2) . . . . . . . . . . . . . . . 9
*Charlie & Flo,* Laurie Graff (2) . . . . . . . . . . . . . . . . . . . . . . . . . 14
*Chicken Shit or Mengele's Mosquito,* Keith Kennedy . . . . . . . 16
*The Connie Saxon Show,* Ethan Kanfer . . . . . . . . . . . . . . . . . . 21
*Dueling Writers,* Mark Bellusci . . . . . . . . . . . . . . . . . . . . . . . . 23
*Echoes from the Street,* Corey Tyler (2) . . . . . . . . . . . . . . . . . . 25
*The Electric Hotdog Machine,* Le Wilhelm . . . . . . . . . . . . . . . 29
*Eve of Crimes: Memory Motel,* Bob Jude Ferrante . . . . . . . . . 31
*The Feast of the Flying Cow...And Other Stories of War,*
 Jeni Mahoney . . . . . . . . . . . . . . . . . . . . . . . . . . . . . . . . . . 33
*Flat Tire,* David Fleisher . . . . . . . . . . . . . . . . . . . . . . . . . . . . . 35
*The Good Daughter,* Dolores Whiskeyman . . . . . . . . . . . . . . 39
*Hanging Lord Haw-Haw*, Jeffrey Hatcher . . . . . . . . . . . . . . . . 40
*Heading West,* Philip Goulding . . . . . . . . . . . . . . . . . . . . . . . 41
*The Invention of Love,* Tom Stoppard (2) . . . . . . . . . . . . . . . . 42
*The Judas Kiss,* David Hare (2) . . . . . . . . . . . . . . . . . . . . . . . . 45
*Just Taking Up Space,* Nancy Gall-Clayton . . . . . . . . . . . . . . . 49
*The Killer and the Comic,* Rooster Mitchell (2) . . . . . . . . . . . . 51
*Listening to Insomnia,* Amy Beth Arkawy . . . . . . . . . . . . . . . . 57
*Louis Slotin Sonata,* Paul Mullin (3) . . . . . . . . . . . . . . . . . . . . 59
*The Martyrdom of Washington Booth,* Jeni Mahoney . . . . . . 66
*The Most Fabulous Story Ever Told,* Paul Rudnick . . . . . . . . . . 67

*New York Actor,* John Guare..........................69
*No One Talks to the Mailman,* Christopher Wall (2).......71
*Perfect World,* Linda Stockham........................74
*The Power of Love,* Sebastian Michael (3)...............76
*A Question of Mercy,* David Rabe (2)...................82
*Rim of the Wheel,* Daphne R. Hull.....................85
*Shoes,* Sky Vogel...................................87
*A Significant Betrayal,* Le Wilhelm (2)..................89
*Sinatragate,* Bob Jude Ferrante.......................94
*Small Mercies,* Heidi Decker (2)......................97
*Sweet Butterfly on an Alligator's Lip,* Richard Lay (3).......101
*Texas,* Judy Soo Hoo...............................104
*Threnody,* David-Matthew Barnes.....................106
*Vernon Early,* Horton Foote..........................108
*What Corbin Knew,* Jeffrey Hatcher...................112
*Wild Man,* Christopher Woods.......................114

Permissions Acknowledgments.......................117

# Foreword

I suppose it's taken me so gosh darn long to complete Smith & Kraus's 1999 scene and monologue books because it was a decade, a century, and indeed a millennium that I was reluctant to see come to an end. But come to an end it has, and here are the very best snippets I could find to help express a collective farewell to a magnificent decade of world theater while at the same time offering an enthusiastic greeting to a brand new age for our incredible dramatic journey.

You men are so hard to shop for. Year after year I struggle not to bring you the same old stuff I found for you last year. Whether or not I manage to succeed is at best a matter of opinion, but I've got to tell you that the search itself is always a life-changing experience for me, and for that I feel that I should close out the century by thanking you for your insatiable need for more monologues.

This year we have some wild offerings indeed. Must have been all of that Millennium Madness and Y2K stuff. . .

Guys looking for edgy, raw, in-your-face material should check out *Chicken Shit* by Keith Kennedy, *The Killer and the Comic* by Rooster Mitchell, *Eve of Crimes: Memory Hotel* by Bob Jude Ferrante, *The Most Fabulous Story Ever Told* by Paul Rudnick, *Texas* by Judy Soo Hoo and *Wild Man* by Christopher Woods.

Those of you who wish to spotlight your dramatic prowess should take a peek at *Vernon Early* by Horton Foote, *Blue Skies Forever* by Claire Braz-Valentine, *Echoes from the Street* by Corey Tyler, *Heading West* by Philip Goulding, *The Judas Kiss* by

David Hare, *Hanging Lord Haw-Haw* by Jeffrey Hatcher, *The Invention of Love* by Tom Stoppard, *Louis Slotin Sonata* by Paul Mullin and *The Feast of the Flying Cow* by Jeni Mahoney.

Rather make 'em laugh than cry? Take a gander at *Listening to Insomnia* by Amy Beth Arkawy, *Flat Tire* by David Fleisher, *New York Actor* by John Guare, *Sinatragate* by Bob Jude Ferrante, *What Corbin Knew* by Jeffrey Hatcher, *Blue Food* by Janice Fronczak and *Dueling Writers* by Mark Bellusci.

There's a lot of great material in this book, and I hope it was worth the wait. . . of course, you're sort of a captive audience, but what the heck, the 2000 books will be here before you know it.

Until then, I wish you all the best. Remember, if you find a monologue that you love, get a copy of the play and read every last word.

May you all suffer thousands upon thousands of broken legs!


Jocelyn Beard

# The Adulterer
Jussi Wahlgren

**Scene:** Helsinki, Finland

**Dramatic**
    Patrik Lindberg (40), a scholar who dreams of freedom while waiting for his wife to die.

    Patrik's wife suffers from a deadly intracranial aneurysm that he is utterly powerless to help her with. Here, he bitterly recounts the demands of a scholar's life and the toll it takes on a marriage.

PATRIK: *(Enters front of stage.)* Let me tell you some facts about a scholar's life. The spouse can take surprisingly well misconducts, negligence, drinking, even violent bursts when the scholar is doing research for her or his doctoral thesis. Oh, those countless nights of horror. Despair, restlessness, mistrust, and skepticism. Oh, those days of hard labor and failure, unlucky experiments and the enormous clinical effort to achieve. What? A piece of paper with lots of unimportant names on it, about what? A trifle, unimportant clarification of a certain enzyme that nobody knows why it's there where it is. And you just make it more complex by not finding out what in the God's name it's supposed to DO there. You know, damned well what I mean. So your spouse understands your frustration and submits her or himself to your agony of struggling against the whole bloody microcosmos. But then! Wow! When the work is finally done and you get your fancy hat and diploma, *then* they're leaving you like badgers leave a burning forest. It's true, someone should do research on that. Maybe they have. Is it better to divorce a doctor of medicine because he earns more? Or because you can brag about it to your friends: I divorced a Ph.D. brain surgeon!

# Bad Buddhists
Robert Vivian

**Scene:** A rundown sleeping room in the dark, withering interior of a major midwestern city.

**Dramatic**
　　Grossman (30s), a man just surviving at society's edge.

　　Grossman suffers horribly from nightmares and is consequently sleep deprived and close to falling into an emotional abyss. His feelings of spiritual despair are exacerbated by the taciturn man who shares his space. Here, Grossman angrily attacks his roommate.

GROSSMAN: It's true. I'm useless for anything that matters.
　　*(Grossman puts his head in his pillow and weeps. The woman enters from right, dressed in a silk nighty. The sound of wind chimes. She kisses Cloudy tenderly. She leaves. Grossman stops crying, wipes his eyes.)*
　　You tell me if there's a god here. You tell me if he visits at night. You tell me. Eh? You of the calm ways. Reaching out for your farm. Life isn't supposed to be this way, is it? You can only work so hard 'til you realize . . . we're never going to make it. My mother said she loved me. You know what I think? I think it's catshit. That's what I think. What's your excuse? *(Silence.)*
　　Yeah, you, Mr. Rumple-Stilt-Skin. Mr. Time-Fuck and his bucket of quarters. His little vegetable garden. If I hear anymore about your goddamned farm, I'm going to rent a bicycle and drive it down your fucking throat. You're fucked. That's what you are. Mr. Innocence. Mr. Do-Not-Wait-Up-For-Me. I don't how the hell we ended up together. Probably some odd little bit of cosmic disaster, a bit of juju. You're just plain fucked in the head, aren't you? You walk around like you're in a dream. Tell you what I think: that's just the fastest fucking way to singing old tunes in your bathroom, bub.

# Blue Food
Janice Fronczak

**Scene:** Here and now

**Serio-comic**
Randy (30–50), a lawyer with an aversion to certain kinds of food.

Here, Randy complains to a coworker about his wife's culinary proclivities.

*(Randy talks to a coworker at a company party about his wife's need to serve him feminine food.)*

RANDY: What color is that? Ugh, no thank you. I don't like to eat blue food. There is something amiss in this world. I come home from a hard day's work and my wife presents me with a cake that she made with a blue teapot on top of it and expects me to be excited. I work with murderers all day and I can't deal with edible teapots when I get home. She meets me at the door with this silly grin on her face wearing an apron from the fifties and drags me into the kitchen to show me her latest creation. I'm under a doctor's care from her last attempt.

Don't get me wrong. I love my wife. For her birthday I got her a series of baking lessons from "Henri." "Henri" is a little frilly man. Come to think of it, ever since those classes I have been fed a lot of pretty, feminine food. Mini-quiches, finger cucumber sandwiches? Huh? Huh?? And I can tell you right now, I don't like it. No sir. Don't like it at all. Look here, is it wrong for me to want manly food? I wear manly clothes, I want manly food. What? Oh, I don't know. Steak, I guess. That really sounds macho, doesn't it? How about homemade lasagna? Things that remind me of my mother. I miss mother. She never fed me blue food.

Mother wants to know why I had to chose such an unfriendly occupation being a lawyer. Criminals are friendly. They are. I caught one bending over talking to a lone pansy sticking out of the concrete the other day. Just talking away. I didn't get too close. I wonder if he would eat a sugar teapot? Probably. My mother never would have dreamed of feeding her "big boy" blue food. Never. Just not manly enough.

# Blue Food
Janice Fronczak

**Scene:** Here and now

**Dramatic**
   Older Man (60–70), a man trying to strike up a conversation.

   Here, a well-meaning senior shares a bad memory of working at a women's prison.

   *(A well-meaning older man approaches two women at a table for simple conversation.)*

OLDER MAN: Here ya' go. *(Gives the two ladies some chocolate kisses.)* You two look like ya' could use a couple of sweets. I can't do sweets hardly anymore. Nope . . . use to be a time I could eat anything I wanted. But, well now . . . nope not anymore. You two look like you're all fussied up for something real special. Not much happens around here, except when they have some trouble up at the prison. Up the road. Ever been in there? I used to work there. No love in there. Naw, no . . . nothin' in there. It's a medium-security joint, but they treat the women there like dogs.
   You look 'em right in the face and there's nobody home. Yep, I used to work maintenance. Cut the lawns. Make everything look real nice. It's funny don't ya think? They care more for the look of the grounds than they do for the souls of those poor women? Some of 'em'll scare you. Ya see, they look like men. That last law they laid down where all the women had to have their hair cut. Whew! That was bad. They cut more than their hair. They cut their "female" away. They say the manager or whoever it is that runs that place don't care for women. No, he don't care for criminals, either. Lock 'em up and throw away the key!

That's why I had to leave. You see, I did care for 'em. Yeah, I still care for 'em.

Well, you ladies enjoy your little chocolate kisses there. Some people . . . well, some folks don't ever get chocolate kisses.

# Blue Food
Janice Fronczak

**Scene:** Here and now

**Dramatic**
  Elderly man (90+), haunted by his wife's tragic drowning in the 1900 Galveston Flood.

  Here, a man who survived one of the worst floods in U.S. history, begs his dead wife for peace.

ELDERLY MAN: She was the most beautiful wife, almost celestial. Stars for eyes and long dark hair you could get lost in. It was the howling wind that scared me. This was no ordinary storm. I knew our beloved Galveston was going under.
  Water started creeping under our front door. Our house was on 31st Street right on the shore. The shore. There was no more shore. Just wave upon wave pounding our beautiful city. Took out all the electricity. The only light was from the lightning when it lit up the sky.
  Honey grew frantic about an elderly cousin of hers. She had to make sure she was alright, she said. I grabbed her wrist and pleaded with her to stay inside safe from the rising water. The last time I saw her she was running down the darkened flooded street. From nowhere a big black monster of a wave crashed into the side of our house and from where I was standing I saw her go under. I was pulled down our chimney and into the water. When I came to I was holding onto part of a neighbor's bench. I thought it was a bench. To my horror I saw that it was my drowned neighbor, Alston. I was too exhausted to scream. In the pitch dark.
  I didn't mind dying. Just didn't want to die alone.
  I still live near the shore. It's there that I see her. Haunting me, haunting the town; in every wave, in every woman's white dress,

in the wind. Why don't the dead leave the living alone? Honey, I'm sorry, I'm sorry! The ocean didn't want me! I'm the one left. At least you're back with the stars.

# Blue Skies Forever
Claire Braz-Valentine

**Scene:** July, 1937

**Dramatic**
George Putnam (50s), Amelia Earhart's husband and manager.

As the world waits anxiously for news of Amelia, George here remembers his first meeting with the famous flier.

GEORGE: *(At center rise.)* The first time I ever saw Amelia Earhardt, I couldn't believe my eyes. It was in Captain Hilton H. Railey's office. We were looking for a lady flier to be the first woman to fly across the Atlantic. The woman we needed wasn't really going to pilot the airplane, just be in it, but she had to be a pilot nonetheless. Had to know the ropes, able to read charts. We interviewed five or six women. Just couldn't find the right one. Then she walked in.

There are some rare and golden times in each of our lives. Times when you know something is happening, something important, that will change you for the rest of your life, for eternity. It's as if some things are written somewhere, and sometimes we get to read them. Sometimes we're shown the truth. When Amelia walked into that office I knew that truth. I was married, a father, a successful publisher, a manager to Charles Lindbergh, an important businessman for God's sake.

I had heard a little about her. She was making a name for herself even then, but I'd never seen a picture of her. I didn't know what to expect. I swear to God, flies could have flown in my mouth, my jaw dropped open so wide. I'll be darned if she didn't look enough like Charles Lindbergh to be his twin sister. She hates people to say that, but that's the God's truth. Well, hell! In walks this angel with the Lindbergh look, yes that's exactly what the press said after the flight, "the Lindbergh look." Of course I gave them the line, but I'll never admit it to Amelia. She was sweet as a kitten with a smile that would charm even the most hardened businessman like me. She has this space between her front teeth. It makes her look sort of vulnerable when she smiles. Most people don't know that. Her public, I mean. Since I've been her manager, I've convinced her to always smile with her mouth closed. She's prettier that way.

Anyway, I said to her, Amelia, what about your family? This is hazardous business. What will they say? And she said to me, "Mr. Putnam. I make my own decisions. And if I decide to pop off in an airplane, then my family won't have any say about it."

# Blue Skies Forever
Claire Braz-Valentine

**Scene:** July, 1937

**Dramatic**
George Putnam (50s), Amelia Earhart's husband and manager.

Sixteen days after Amelia's plane, the Electra, is reported missing in the Pacific, George defends himself against those who held him responsible for the tragedy.

GEORGE: Each day is a year. Each minute drags on into agony. For sixteen days we have conducted the most extensive rescue attempt ever for a lost plane. There have been 10 ships, 65 airplanes, and 4000 men in the Pacific. The aircraft carrier *Lexington,* three battleships, three destroyers, two Japanese naval vessels, and a British freighter, and nothing. No trace. And today Naval authorities announce the search is over. Just like the that! It's over. Well, I've got news for them. This search is not over. Not if I have anything to say about it. This is not just some chump pilot we are talking about here. This is Amelia Earhart Putnam. *(Very angry.)* And they better get one thing straight about George Putnam, and get it straight right now! I did not put in all these years for nothing. They think they can just give me the bum's rush and people are going to just forget about Amelia? Not on my life. Not if I have anything to say about it. *(Walks over to chair and sits.)*

I'm not going to take this lying down. I've got all of her notes, all her flight logs, and all her phone calls to me during the flight on tape. I've got access to almost everything she's written. I know every story she ever told, things about her even her mother doesn't know. I've got them! And if they think with just this proclamation, they are going to sweep her memory under the rug, then they got another thing coming. Amelia was the bravest woman in the history of the world, and America will remember her. Mark my words. They will remember her.

When she was a little girl she would read adventure books. And everyone of those books were about boys. And when she finished the book she would be filled with sadness because she was a girl and girls didn't have adventures. She said once the main mistake she ever made was being born a girl, because that made everything she ever wanted to do so difficult. There were never any books for her. There was no one telling her it was okay for her to have adventures. Well *I* said it was okay. I told her, "Go ahead. If you want to fly the Pacific Ocean, fly it. I'll be there for you when you come back. You want to fly the Atlantic Ocean? Fine, do it. I'll be there for you." And I was. Waiting there in the airports, in the middle of winter, in the middle of the night. I sailed halfway around the world to just be there when she landed, anywhere, soaked to my skin and freezing . . . but what the Hell. I would go anywhere to be there for her. To let her know it was okay. *(Getting angry.)* I was nothing, less than nothing. I was introduced at parties as Mr. Earhart. So what did I care? So what did I care if the press called me pushy? So fine. It makes for a good story. And if those suckers didn't see that all I wanted for Amelia was a good story, then they're as stupid as I always thought they were. I know what they called me. You've heard it, too. The "lens louse!" They think I don't know that. Because I wanted to be photographed with my wife! Is that so awful? So what if her friends don't like me. They think I'm a schemer or overbearing. Well, screw them. It isn't about liking me. It was about Amelia, always about Amelia.

I gave her everything I had. I was the best manager she could have ever had. I made every deal work. All she had to do was ask me. She wanted it, she got it. A new car? Fine, what color? A new house? No problem, how many rooms? Sixteen? Fine. A new plane? A brand new Goddamn plane, bigger than anything she ever even dreamed of? Sure, just leave it to G.P. G.P. can do it. G.P. can do anything. *(Puts his head in his hands—suddenly in tears.)* G.P. can do anything. Except get Amelia back. G.P. can't get Amelia back.

*(Pulls himself together with great effort. Gets up walks around.)*

*(Suddenly very angry.) I* simply do not understand how something so stupid like a Goddamned radio frequency could have gotten so screwed up. And I know certain people are going to shoot their mouths off about why we didn't install a radio transmitter on Howland Island. I'm just waiting for that. They're not fooling me. People just don't understand our schedules, that with the time that would have taken it would have messed up publication of her new book for the Christmas sale. She would never have made that deadline if we had any more delays. We had enough delays. It was important to us. And I told her that. She could have asked for a radio man on the island to send signals, sure. But she didn't want him. She said she didn't need it. We asked her and she said no. *She* said no! Not me! And then, when the Itasca couldn't track her, and they sent a man to the island with a high-frequency radio, the batteries went dead. The Goddamned batteries! I can't believe this. How could this have happened? But none of this would have made any difference. She simply didn't stay on the radio long enough for anyone to get a fix on her. Anyway, why do you have a navigator on a plane in the first place? Why don't people understand this? *(Turns to audience with cold hard anger.)* There is no proof that any more expense on the trip, either with extra personnel or more equipment, would have made any difference. No proof at all! And I will not have people pointing their fingers at *me. (Yelling at audience—very angry.) It is not my fault.*

# Charlie & Flo
Laurie Graff

**Scene:** The Bronx, 1965

**Dramatic**
>Jerry (40s), a high school shop teacher who has started to date a student's mother.
>
>Here, well-meaning Jerry confronts Charlie, whose mother he is dating and offers a sympathetic ear.

JERRY: That's a good plan. You know that expression? You want to make God laugh, tell him your plans. I lost my father too. It was during the Depression. I was around your age. I was at school that day. Thomas Jefferson High School, in Brooklyn. The East New York section. The principal came into the classroom and asked for me. Everyone looked. I was sure something great had happened and I had won some big award. At that time I was planning on becoming a doctor. My father wanted it very much. He was a barber. He learned the trade in the old country. His name was Nat, short for Nathan. *(In Yiddish accent, pretending to be Nathan, extending his arm for a handshake.)* "Nat, the barber from Romania." Fifteen cents for a haircut and a shave, and with that he supported our family. On his feet all day, his fingers ached from holding the scissors. He wanted better for me. I walked with Mr. Hillman down the stairwells and through the hall into his office. My mother was sitting there crying with my little sister Ruth. "Your father," my mother said. That was all she had to say. He was at work. A heart attack. I obviously didn't become a doctor. I want to Brooklyn College so I could be nearby. I had to work to be around for Ruthie, help my mother. My mother passed on two years ago. I always took care of her. She didn't get to see my sister Ruthie's son Bar Mitzvahed last week. But she knew we were okay. You see, Charlie. I know what it's like. That's why I'd like to be a special kind of friend to you. Maybe, kind of like . . .

# Charlie & Flo
Laurie Graff

**Scene:** The Bronx, 1965

**Dramatic**
Charlie (17), a high school senior who has been keeping a secret.

Charlie has known that he was offered a full scholarship to Cornell University for quite some time. Here, he finally tells his mother.


CHARLIE: I got a scholarship.
[FLO: What??]
CHARLIE: A full scholarship. To Cornell.
[FLO: Why didn't you tell me?]
CHARLIE: I wanted to tell you. I came home. It was the night you came home screaming because the supermarket was out of the Yerzheit candles, and you wanted to light one for Dad. I was really excited to tell you, but you were angry 'cause I had the guys over and we were playing football in the living room. And then I forgot to shut the windows and it rained in, and I forgot to defrost, and you just kept yelling at me. Then, a few days later, I went into the kitchen to tell you, after you did the dishes. And you were sitting there talking to the empty Yetzheit glass—one we keep for juice—and you were telling Dad you were happy about C.C.N.Y. because you didn't want to be alone. *And* you didn't tell him about Mr. Bernstein. I felt really bad for you. I didn't want to tell you I wanted to go away. *(Pause.)* I'm going to Cornell, Ma. It's gonna be great for me and I'm going. But I love you. And I'll come home from the holidays.

# Chicken Shit or Mengele's Mosquito

Keith Kennedy

**Scene:** Here and now

**Serio-comic**

Rex (20–30), a man who has decided to become a chicken in the name of animal rights.

Rex has discovered an unusual kinship with chickens during a nighttime liberation raid on a huge chicken farm. In fact, he is becoming a chicken. Rex is plagued however, by a disturbing and allegorical dream that compares the life of a chicken to that of any being who is systematically tortured and killed by a fascist regime.

REX: My mind has lost its edge! *(Pause.)* It has to be fine-tuned—and it's not. *(In a frenzy.)* It's blocked—*(Choking.)*—by the dream!
*(He rocks back on his heels in despair.)*
Always the same!
*(As he closes his eyes, there comes the distant echo of a train's steam whistle.)*
*(Testily.)* Always the same bloody dream!
*(The clanking of goods wagons rumbling. He opens his eyes. Combatively.)* And I am always there! *(Angrily.)* Me! *(He thrusts forward aggressively.)* Understand this—we are talking chicken, here. *(Pause.)* This is my dream—and I am there—with my kind! *(Pause.)*
*(He listens.)*
—all my kin are there.
*(A murmuration of feathered creatures.)*
*(Bitterly.)* In their hundreds—their thousands—
*(The train noises rise.)*
We are all—

*(The wagon wheels thunder and slowly fade until he is left in silence.)*

—in line— *(He laughs harshly.)* —for the experience of a lifetime. *(He steps forward and stretches his wings as if to ease cramped muscles.)*

It is a beautiful day— *(Bitterly)* —it always is! *(Pause.)* A lovely day for mankind, and chickens, too. one of such richness that, stretch out—

*(He snakes out his left hand, fingers palping the air, and simultaneously, beats his right wing.)*

*(Looking from hand to wing and back.)* Within the span of an arm or a wing—

*(He lowers both.)* —a finger or a pin—the free, fresh air is there to be grabbed, and it's so sweet and balmy—and yet— *(He utters a dispirited squawk.)* —on this platform, there is only one-way traffic. (Dully.) Follow the yellow, brick road to where our captors are ready to go about their daily business. *(Angrily.)* Forget the sunshine—who needs that kiss of life when—

*(He dissolves into a fuming, speechless rage and squawks savagely, but his feet move.)*

*(Struggling to contain his anger.)* By now, we are moving down the platform toward the uniformed figures. I try to hold back— *(He slackens his step.)* —try to swim against the tide, and I ask myself "What are we doing?" *(Pause, slowly.)* "What—are—we—doing?" *(Pause.)* That is how it always is in my dream. I ask the question and—a *(Pause.)* —I always get the same answer. *(Pause.)* They are going to their deaths—*(With incredulity.)* —with dignity!

*(He stares at the audience without speaking.)*

They are going to die like chickens, and— *(his voice wavers and drops.)* —that— *(he pauses.)* —is not how it should be.

*(He writhes in disgust.)*

Yet, I move— *(His feet move.)* –the others are moving. But—a *(He chirrups.)* —as I go I gather my wits. *(Pause.)* Why me? Why am I here? *(Pause.)* Not to die? *(Pause.)* I can't accept that! No—but— *(Irritably.)* —the sun is scorching now—the peak caps are getting closer and—and— *(Viciously.)* —suddenly, I know! *(Pause.)* Damn the sun to hell with the evil games they are playing—

*(He squawks triumphantly.)*

I have a smart card or two to play. *(He clucks with self-satisfaction.)* They aren't aces, but they could prove to be a winning combination. *(He halts.)* If you take aces as Love— *(He hesitates.)* –call this precious pair Memory—and Hate— *(He crows menacingly.)* –an explosive mix—

*(He resumes his shuffling advance.)*

—as any human knows! *(He laughs, then chirrups.)* Remember battery born—I wasn't! I'm no pure White Wyandotte or Light Sussex— *(He chuckle-chirrups again.)* —I'm a new breed—

*(He stiffens and stops and peers intently ahead.)*

—and the Memory card comes first. *(Furiously.)* It is him! *(Pause.)* I know the figure in the center of their circle. *(Pause.)* The maniac with the monocle. *(Pause, sententiously.)* I read my history books at school. *(Pause, slowly.)* And the baton in his hand with which he is conducting—oh, yes—

*(He jerks from side to side.)*

—right—left—right—tick—tock—orchestrating—

*(He squawks viciously.)*

—death—it is the man! It is the same—

*(He squawks again.)*

—and I am powerfully built for a bird—a hybrid! And I am ready to remake history—I am, and— *(He squints ahead.)* —the eyes have it! I shall go for his eyes—

*(All his movements become tempered with caution.)*

*(Whispering.)* —I shall— *(He darts a glance at the audience and reverts to his normal voice level.)* —and I always do, in each dream—

*(His pace slackens.)*

*(Breathlessly.)* I draw close. I can see his stick ticking like a metronome—and the peak of his cap flashing in the sunlight as he conducts—

[MEN: Rechts—links—links—links—rechts—links—]

REX: —right—left—left—and— *(He gags with excitement.)* —I think again and decide to go for his throat, and— *(He squawks.)* —I have the strength, I'm sure of it. I feel an excitement of a kind never felt before. (He crows exultantly.) Here it comes—The Avenging Chicken meets The Angel of Death! *(He laughs.)* I am ready and more than willing. *(Pause.)* I am eager. And I am sure it can be done—and will be well done, and— *(He fumbles for words.)* —shouldn't it have been done before—in a real time— Beaten to the punch. *(Pause.)* I—I—

*(He struggles to shape his next statement.)*

—to kill a man is one thing. *(Pause.)* To kill a mosquito is—

*(He twitches uncomfortably.)*

—I know that in the natural order of things, I should, quite easily, be able to— *(Pause.)* —but—but—being the kind of animal I am—

*(He shrugs helplessly and laughs uneasily.)*

You must have got my measure by now what I am—a sort of politicized chicken, yes? And—yet— *(Falteringly.)* —here—here is— *(With an upsurge of confidence.)* —a fellow winged warrior at work—going about my business! *(He laughs loudly.)* Similar goals—what else? *(Pause.)* But—

*(He looks expectantly at the audience.)*

—so much better equipped than myself. *(Pause.)* No card-carrying amateur! *(Admiringly.)* A true professional, you might say. This tiny airborne creature with all kingdoms terrestrial after its blood— *(Pause.)* —taking the fight to the enemy! *(Pause.)* I like it. *(Pause.)* There was I, about to tear flesh and suffer for it at the hands of the doctor's henchmen—and— *(Enthusiastically.)* —one tiny puncture—oh—oh—

*(He waves his arms extravagantly.)* I like it—I like it!

An invisible, deadly seed for the Doctor!

*(He shoots out his arms as if they were antennae and buzzes fiercely.)*

ZZZzzzzzHHHHHHH!! *(He whoops with glee.)* Oh, only connect!

*(Suddenly, his zizzing is drowned by the throbbing, high-pitched drone of the mosquito of his dreams. He tries to*

*escape, but this dominant buzz compels him to continue his mimicry. Finally, the noise fades. He shrinks back.)*
*(In a troubled voice.)* Of course, I exaggerate. I—
*(He starts forward, stops, and listens intently. Hearing nothing he turns, again, to the audience.)*

I got carried away. *(He laughs in embarrassment.)* Impersonations were my specialty at school. So— *(Uneasily.)* —I'll spare you—

*(He freezes. A residual buzz is heard, briefly.)*

*(Hurriedly.)* I'll spare you more. *(Pause.)* But—it was necessary to show you—because—this is the threat.

*(His face twists in frustration.)*

—to—oh—well— *(Nervously.)* —to my chickenhood— *(Quickly.)* —to my newly found peace of mind. *(Helplessly.)* That's what really matters. *(Resolutely.)* Now, it has to be a case of— "Chicken! I stick!" *(Despair.)* Believe me, I want no more identity crises in my life.

# The Connie Saxon Show
Ethan Kanfer

**Scene:** American suburbia circa 1960, or thereabouts

**Serio-comic**
   Hedgehog (12–16), a boy whose mother has just suffered a nervous breakdown.

   Here, poor Hedgehog presents a report on an extremely difficult topic (to wit: love) to his class at school.

HEDGEHOG: Hi, um. This is kind of an extra-credit assignment type thing. It's about that poem that we read on Tuesday, called "Love is not All: It is not Meat or Drink" . . . or rutabagas. *(Snickers.)* Sorry. *(Clears throat.)* One of the key stanzas of this poem, by Edna Ste. Vincent Millay, goes thusly; "Love cannot fill the thickened lung with breath, \ Nor clean the blood, nor set the fractured bone; \ Yet many a man is making friends with death \ Even as I speak, for lack of love alone." . . . What do these words mean? This essayist—does not know. Except for the making friends with death part. I think—I mean one thinks, that having death for a buddy would be real good, 'cause then one could go anywhere and say anything one wanted and nobody'd pick a fight with one. . . . I guess that sounded pretty dumb. Anyway, the question is, can love cure you when you're sick? Well, my—someone this essayist kind of knows real well is in the hospital, but one's not allowed to see her yet. So I guess you do need doctors and pills and stuff instead of—
   *(He sees something offstage and makes a fist.)*
   Murphy you—I mean one better quit makin' that face or this essayist is gonna give one a knuckle sandwich after school! . . . *(Clears throat.)* In conclusion, it is . . . um . . . Look, the whole point of this thing was to basically punish this essayist for saying

that love was dumb. Alright, one's sorry one said that. It's not dumb, it's important, at least that's what grown-ups think.

*(As he talks, he begins folding his notes into a paper airplane, as Flukev has taught him.)*

I guess I just don't know why anybody'd wanna write a poem about it. Especially when there's all this other stuff to do like playing ball and catching fireflies . . . Maybe she wrote it on a rainy day, I don't know. Or maybe it's 'cause it's a girl that wrote it. A lady, I mean. Poetess . . . But even girls like to skip rope and play jacks and hopskotch and stuff . . . Well, I guess I got an F. I'll see you guys at detention.

# Dueling Writers
Mark Bellusci

**Scene:** A restaurant

**Serio-comic**
   Phil (20s–30s), a frustrated writer.

   When his writing partner accepts a job in advertising, Phil accuses her of selling out. When she asks how his screenplays are doing, he offers the following sarcastic reply.

PHIL: Well, I'm re-setting a lot of my screenplays to places like, Victorian England, the Amish Country—artsy places like that.
[LAUREN: But what about plots, how you changing those?]
PHIL: Well, I'm using this writing technique an old professor gave me. See, the trick is to try to flesh out a kid's nursery rhyme without changing its innocent tone. I've been fleshing out the old Humpty Dumpty story. *(Phil pulls out his notes.)* You want to hear it?
[LAUREN: Sure.]
PHIL: *(He stands up to give the following monologue. He emphasizes the egg words throughout.)* This story is told by Humpty's best friend, OverEasy Ed. "I don't give a shit about the soft hay," Humpty told me. "I don't give a shit about the heat lamps. I wanna get out of this friggin' cubicle. I wanna live, man." "But Hump," I said, "your old man hears you're heading out, he'll kick the shit out of you." "Hey, how's he gonna know?" he said. "He's always out, hanging out with the young chicks. He don't give a shit about me. If he hadn't laid that golden egg, we'd be livin' in a poor house anyway." Well, I laughed right at him. Said everybody should have it so good, being a rich egg and everything. So he says he'd give it all up in a second if he wasn't so raw! "If I could just get that hard-boiled treatment," he said, "then I wouldn't have to be cooped up in here anyway." Well I

told him, I said, "you ain't hard-boiled. And if you screw around, you're gonna spring a leak, then good-bye." So you know what he says? He says, "Maybe it would be better that way. You think I don't hear all those hard-boiled guys on the corner, snickering at me. You don't think I hear them saying, "Look at that soft-boiled wimp, bein' pulled in that cushioned wagon." Why don't you come out and scramble with the hard-boileds?" I asked him why he listened to them anyway? They're old, you know? Getting that smell, that rotten smell. What they wouldn't do for that refrigeration treatment Hump was getting. Then he barked that the refrigeration thing is bullshit! What the hell are they preserving me for? I'd rather go out in a blaze of splatter than where I am now. So he bolts up to go, but I stopped him. I wanted to know how he was gonna get past the guards at the gate. So he says we wasn't going through the gate. Says he's going over the wall, they'll never know he left. Well, that was the last I ever saw of him. Now when I get lonely, I just look at that little piece of shell I've got on my mantelpiece.

*(Pause.)*

[LAUREN: *(With heavy sarcasm.)* Oh yeah, that technique worked.]

PHIL: *(In love with his work, oblivious to Lauren's sarcasm.)* It's called, "Nursery Rhymes from the Gutter."

[LAUREN: How anyone could come up with a Goodfellas version of Humpty Dumpty is beyond me.]

PHIL: You think it's got a chance?

# Echoes from the Street
Corey Tyler

**Scene:** Here and now

**Dramatic**
The Father (40–50), a man whose son has been murdered.

Here, a grieving father explains how he is able to forgive those who murdered his son.

THE FATHER: *"And on that blessed day, we will be caught up to meet him . . . in the twinkling of an eye . . . "*
People ask me how? How can I do it? How can I forgive? How can I live my life from day to day and not hate the ones that took my son away from me? And I tell them, by the grace of God.

There's no more room in my life for anger. No more room inside of me for hate. I wanted so much to be angry at the ones that killed him. But I spent so much of my life that way for all the things I thought God had done to me . . . that I forgot how to live. So many years I wasted angry. So much time I let slip past . . . all because I didn't know the way God works. Because I didn't know that heartache and pain aren't in our lives to cause us pain but strengthen our faith. That loss and hardship . . . and even death, aren't meant to punish us . . . but bring us closer to his will.

He was such a beautiful boy. No matter what they say about him . . . he was precious to me . . . to both of us. The first time I ever held him I knew what all the pain in my life was for. Every burden I'd ever carried brought me to that moment. Standing in the delivery room . . . holding everything I'd ever hoped for in my arms. He was all the proof I needed that there was a God . . . and that there had been a plan for my life all along. That I wasn't suffering all those years for nothing.

I realized that we are all just as beautiful in God's eyes as my son was to me. In that moments, I found the answer to every question I ever screamed at God the moment. He was the reason why. I had to be ready for him.

So I can't be angry now, because I know the way God works. I know that this was his plan for my son's life. And I know that God in all his wisdom doesn't give us what we can't handle. And whatever he does give us, he uses to make us stronger. Even if it means burying your only son.

That verse speaks of the day when all God's children are caught up to spend eternity in Heaven. That's what keeps me now . . . knowing that day will come. Knowing that just the way I held his body in my arms, his spirit rests in the arms of God. Knowing he is loved without limits . . . far away from the anger and the violence of this world.

Although I have the burden of living without the sight of his smile or the sound of his voice . . . I know he's with the father. And I know the day will come when I see my son again. And it will happen ". . . *in the twinkling of an eye* . . . "

# Echoes from the Street
Corey Tyler

**Scene:** Here and now

**Dramatic**
 Murderer (20–30).

Here, a young sociopath reveals his barren soul.

THE MURDERER: I am what you think I am. I am everything you think I should be. You speak of me in circles, in fear or in disgust. I am the embodiment of your judgment or compassion, your dreams or your disdain. Your fondest wish or your deepest fear. For you see, I am a murderer.

I was born into the world a bastard. Stripped of the natural crown of a father's name. Nursed through infancy by a mother no more than a child herself. The common traits of warmth and safety were absent in my childhood. In their place were stripped walls and shattered windows. Burned out cars in empty lots. Sidewalks cluttered with empty cans and corners draped with haggard men. Their young faces hardened from lives lived without purpose.

I dangled from my days of youth on moments made from coarse connections. To be hungry meant to eat and to eat meant to steal. To live meant to survive and to survive meant to fight. I began to wander the streets of my neighborhood at night. Meeting with others who were as bruised and weakened by that force we could not explain, the aching pulse of the world's disgust. We began to travel in something of a pack . . . like stalking wolves in the hours past dusk. Running from the hate the world had to offer toward the destruction it assumed.

We were mercenaries without purpose, villains without cause. Pillaging the world that wronged us. We would write our names in spray paint on the sides of buildings long abandoned so that the world would know that we were here and had lived. When the need was fit to warrant we robbed the handbags of women old enough to have nursed us. Using our earnings to purchase delusions. Drugs, drink . . . anything to drown the voices in our heads. The voices telling us our lives were being wasted running from what we could not escape, the truth of our worthlessness.

And as the pain of my life continued, my heart began to swell with a rage without regret. An anger that turned my thoughts toward Vengeance. Vengeance from those who dammed. Vengeance from those who'd scorned. *Vengeance* . . . from those who left me with so little that was right and wondered why so much I did was wrong. And then, that night, I saw him. The boy. I struck him with my fists . . . watching the bicycle fall beside him from the blow. He screamed from the ground, crying for his life beneath the boots and fists that kicked the hope and promise from his eyes. And then, I reached back, taking the gun from my waist . . . and fired.

*(A gunshot is heard.)*

I stood there in the silence, staring at the thin strands of blood that ran beneath my feet. That night, that need, that lasting thirst for vengeance of the world's denial I quenched in the instant of a gunshot's echo. Leaving in the boy's body on that corner in the night what was left as my birthright . . . nothing.

Now there are those who will say that I am nothing less than a monster. A derelict worthy only of your disdain. A tragedy, a symptom or even a victim. They will say that I am a murderer. But I will tell you what I am . . . if you haven't figured it already.

I am what you think I am. I am everything you think I should be. I am the embodiment of your judgment or your compassion. Your fondest wish or deepest fear. And if my reason has yet to make you believe, then I ask you . . . look into the eyes of your children. Look at how they run from you . . . traveling in packs like stalking wolves in the hours past dusk. Look into the eyes of your children. Do you know who I am now?

# The Electric Hot Dog Machine
Le Wilhelm

**Scene:** An apartment, 1971

**Serio-comic**
   Bert (20–30), a bit of a geek who talks too much. Wants to be cool.

   Bert is a small-time drug dealer and stoner who works as the doorman at the local movie theater. While getting high with friends, Bert here explains why he doesn't mind selling concessions at the kiddie shows.

BERT: I like kids. So it ain't so bad for me, but it drives most people batty. One night they's playing some horror show and it wasn't doing well and so . . . I was supposed to be tearing tickets, and you can be pretty ripped if all you have to do is tear tickets. So I took some acid. Some of the Purple Dragon stuff they had a few years back. I get to work and the boss he says one of the chicks that works the concession ain't showing up so I got to work the concession and for some reason we get real busy. And I'm ripped to the gills. And I have no idea how many people there were there, but it seemed liked thousands, it was like I was in a crowd scene of a Cecil B. DeMille movie. And they're screaming, screaming, on one side they scream popcorn and on the other side they scream Coca Cola. And I'm just working as fast as I can. I'm giving them Coca Colas, and I'm buttering their popcorn. And it's hell, but I'm handling it. Then I look over at this damn hot dog machine. It's one of them electric jobs. You stick the wiener on the prong and then they turn round and round 'til the wiener gets roasted. But the problem with them is they don't stop when the wiener's done. The heat stops or cools off, but the machine just keeps turning, just keeps going round and round. And I start looking at it and off in the distance I hear the crowd from the

DeMille movie calling popcorn, popcorn, butterfinger, baby ruth, Coca Cola, but I can't move, I'm totally mesmerized by that hot dog going round and round. I can't stop looking. I just can't stop looking. I'm waiting. You know what I'm waiting for? I'm waiting for someone to come and buy a hot dog. And then someone says hot dog please. And I hear this music like something, you'd hear in the *Greatest Story Ever Told* or in the *Song of Bernadette* and I take the hot dog and I put mustard and catsup and relish on it and I'm free. But then the girl working with me puts another wiener on the prong . . . and it all starts over again.

*(A moment. Bert is embarrassed and everyone is a little quiet, a little stoned and a little nonplussed).*

Well, I got to be going. I got a deal I got to finish.

# Eve of Crimes: Memory Hotel

Bob Jude Ferrante

**Scene:** A motel room

**Dramatic**

Dylan (29), a lit fuse in a world made of nitrate compounds, a killer.

Here, a man whose life has been defined by violence tells the tale of his first kill.

DYLAN:
I remember the first guy I offed. I was . . . what? Nineteen? Workin' for Kinneally. Dogface Kinneally. The guy, his name was . . . Clark . . . Clark Whitebread or something . . . was behind on his payment.

[TABITHA:
*(Turns on the water. Stares at herself in the mirror.)*
Here we go. True confessions.]

I mean, Clark Whitebread, what kind of moron would get behind on a loan to a brick wall like Kinneall?

So they said, "Shake him down. Don't off him. Shake him up."

[TABITHA:
*(To herself.)* I dunno, guess morons are your field of expertise.]

I get the address, this hotel by the airport. Zip the lock, slip in. *(Shouts.)* "Hey, freeze mo'fuggah!"

Everything's going great. I'm scaring the living shit outa Clark, waving my gun around. It's great.

Clark, the stupid WASP bastard! He's got a gun. This little tiny nickel-plated Wyatt Earp gun. Hidden. In the bed rail. And his weight is pushing the mattress into the bedrail. It's stuck.

Blam, blam, blam! One less stupid son of a bitch in the world. No death scene. Just a cold dead body.

If it's you or them, only one winner is possible.

[TABITHA:
*(To herself.)* "Waving my gun around." "Whoop de doo." *(Splashes water on her face; her eyes fill with water and makeup, which stings.)*]

[Ow, Ow, Ow, Ow!
*(Tries to yank the towel from the rack. It won't budge. Addresses the towel.)*
Come on, come on, bastard.]

[*(She yanks the towel off the rack; the towel bar breaks off and clangs to the floor.)*]

# The Feast of The Flying Cow... And Other Stories of War

Jeni Mahoney

**Scene:** The apartment of Anya and Izak Andonov in a country torn apart by civil war

**Dramatic**
 Izak (30–40), a man whose life has been all but destroyed by war.

 Izak has been hiding in his bathroom for quite some time. The unexpected arrival of a relief worker has brought him back to life, so to speak. Here, he says a heartfelt grace as he and his wife prepare to enjoy the meal provided by the relief worker.

IZAK: Do you know what I wish? *(He pauses.)* I wish that it were harder to kill a man.
[NILES: What kind of wish is that?]
[AUDREY: Yes, it's a bit vulgar isn't it?]
IZAK: It just think it should take more effort. Not just this tool, this gun, to point and pull. We should have to chase each other down like animals and tear the enemy's flesh with our nails and teeth— hunt for the vein that will empty our combatant's body fastest. Feel their blood in our mouths, their skin and muscle and soul. The price of that life should be one of total exhaustion. The victor should stumble home filthy and wasted, having to sleep for days. He should wake up with sore muscles and scrapped joints that send shooting pains through the body for weeks as a reminder. Each time flashing us back to a moment, a blow, a bite. A physical memory of each life taken. Something that rushes like a wave over the body. A shudder so strong that it may hemorrhage us completely. This is where mankind fails. We live with our heads, think of it. Yes THINK. We depend on this to make us

great, the most powerful animal in the world. We can cover the earth with asphalt ten time times over, what great animals we are! We found a way to kill each other without more than the jump of a synapse. Pull the trigger. There, it's done. Close your eyes. Walk away. Close your eyes. It tastes like chicken.

*(Holds a piece of stew up to Niles. Niles stares strangely at Izak. Izak's stomach begins to turn. He puts the meat back into the bowl and crosses away from the table. He recovers himself and laughs slightly.)*

My own wish, and I haven't the stomach for it. But I'm glad of that. I am.

# Flat Tire
David Fleisher

**Scene:** A roadside

**Serio-comic**

Dexter (20s–30s), a young man frustrated with his inability to change a flat tire.

Dexter's ex-girlfriend, Beth, left him for an auto mechanic, so when his car breaks down with a flat his lack of car-repair skill leads him to leave an angst-ridden stream-of-consciousness message on her answering machine.

DEXTER: Testing . . . testing. Okay, I was driving down the road when all of a sudden I hear this horrible noise. Sounded like a gunshot. The car starts to weave every witcha way, and I almost drove into a canal. I managed to pull over into a ditch . . . got out and immediately saw I had a flat tire.
*(Pause.)*
Beth, as I record this I'm standing next to the tire in question . . . the car . . . well, I don't know where the hell it is, and frankly I don't care. The sun is shining, birds singing, air feels . . . strike that . . . strike all that. Beth, I need to tell you something. It's been gnawing away at my insides for quite some time. I want you to know the truth about me . . . all of it . . . I'm gonna just come right out and say it. I know things are a little different between us now, but still you deserve to know who I really am.
I get the feeling you'd like me to be some sort of Renaissance man, you know, do *anything*, if I set my mind to it. Well, Beth, I know myself, and that's just not gonna happen. This tire lying next to me?
*(Pause.)*
*Why* do you think it's lying next to me?
*(Shouting at tape recorder.)*

Because I don't know what to do with it!
*(Stares at recorder a moment.)*
Again? Fine.
*(Shouting.)*
I do not know how to change a flat tire!

Okay? In fact, I have *never* been able to change a flat tire. Remember a month ago, Beth, when I called you from a pay phone and said I'd be late for dinner 'cause I was changing a tire on the Interstate? That was a lie. I was having my car washed. I don't know how to check my oil. I don't know how to put water in the radiator. I don't even know where the radiator is. And you know what else, Beth? I have absolutely no idea how to install an air filter. In fact, I didn't know until recently that cars even *had* air filters. I don't know the difference between a carburetor and a crank shaft.

See, Beth, in this society men are expected to know about all that stuff. Now just hear me out . . . God knows when I'll get up the nerve to be this candid again. The typical "90's Woman" wants to be free and independent . . . say *fuck* just like the men. But you know what I think? Deep down, Beth, a woman, *any* woman, including you, if given the choice, and I'll get specific here, would rather *not* change a flat tire. Oh, sure, she may take out the jack, roll up her sleeves . . . you know, she's being independent and all. But you know what she's really thinking? Why doesn't that mothball-boyfriend-of-mine get over here?!

Look, I know you've met a zillion guys—*one* guy in particular, and I'll get to him in a minute—they can all change a tire with both hands tied behind their backs. Oh, I've met the type, believe me.

*(Stares at tape recorder.)*

What's all this got to do with us?! Beth, heh-loh? If I can't perform the most basic male task of changing a tire, it begs the question: What *else* can't I do? Will I be able to fix the lawnmower when it gets broken? No. Will I be able to fix your hair dryer when it breaks? Don't count on it. Will I be able to fix the reading light on your side of the bed when it falls off? I don't *think* so. And speaking of the bed, will I be able to satisfy you sexually?

*(Stares at recorder a few moments.)*

We were lucky that time.

Beth, let me ask you something. Do you have any idea what it feels like . . . I mean, for me personally . . . to be standing next to this tire? One word. Degrading.

*(Kicks tire.)*

. . . it's flat . . . I can't fix it. So here I am. All alone. God knows where. No one to talk to. Suffering. That's right, Beth, suffering.

*(Kicks tire, repeatedly.)*

. . . all because of this son-of-a-bitchin' tire! And I don't even have the balls to tell you about it in person. I'm sending you a tape because I'm too embarrassed to look you in the eye. Now I ask you: Are those the actions of a man . . . a real man? I don't *think* so.

I can just see us married. Take our honeymoon! We're getting ready for bed, you're dressed in a silk negligee, we throw the covers back, you climb into bed and throw your arms out for me to join you. Then an expression of awareness spreads over your face; suddenly, you remember something and whisper softly to me: "Honey, you're an intelligent, sweet, compassionate man . . . but . . . well, let's face it, you're no Antonio Banderas."

*(Sits on tire.)*

Beth, I love you. You're the only woman I've ever really cared about. I want to spend the rest of my life with you. I want you to be just as proud of me as I am of you. But how can you? What are you gonna tell your girlfriends? "Dexter's generous and successful and loving . . . but . . . well, he has this problem."

*(Silence.)*

I knew sooner or later you'd end up dating someone else. Disappointed and hurt? Sure. Wouldn't you be? But a car mechanic? Why a mechanic for God's sake?!

*(Pause.)*

That second time we went out . . . the car started smoking.

Remember? You didn't say one word to me, not one word, when I couldn't figure out how to open the hood. I saw the way you looked at me, Beth, I knew exactly what you were thinking:

*(Stares at recorder.)*

"I'll bet he has a hard time getting it up."

But I warned you, didn't I? Our very first date? I told you I'm not a macho kinda guy, a jack-of-all-trades, a Mister *fix-it*. And you said . . . I remember this like it was yesterday . . . you said, "Who cares? I just wanna be with a guy who's smart and sensitive." Smart and sensitive?

*(Staring at tape recorder.)*

Beth, you're dating a guy who opens beer cans with his teeth and has a tattoo on his arm that says guard dog!

*(Silence.)*

Look at me . . . talking to a tape recorder. And where are *you* right now, if you don't mind me asking? With Guard Dog? Asshole's probably showing you how to rotate his tires.

Look, Beth, I'm sorry for losing my temper. Doesn't matter anyway. This will be the last time you hear my voice. It's just not worth it anymore.

*(Kicks tire.)*

This is the last straw.

*(He takes out a gun and stares a few moments at the tape recorder and tire. He tries to work the gun, but it jams. He continues to fiddle with it, hitting it, etc., until he finally throws it down. He takes out a pocketknife and begins jabbing the tire, repeatedly.)*

Happy now? Huh? You son-of-a-bitch!

*(As he continues to stab the tire, his cellular phone rings.)*

*(Into phone.)* Hello? Stop crying first. I can't understand a thing you're saying.

*(Pause.)*

Sweetheart, didn't I tell you dating a mechanic's not all it's cracked up to be?

# The Good Daughter
Dolores Whiskeyman

**Scene:** After World War I. Northwestern Missouri along the Missouri River

**Dramatic**
 Rudy (60s), a tenant farmer.

 Rudy and his wife, Rachel are trying to live the tough uncompromising life of farmers. When Rachel loses their first child, Rudy angrily confronts her father who promised that he would one day take over the family farm and tells him that he wants to give up.

RUDY: I heard everythin' you said for way too long. Ain't nothin' turned out the way you said. Nothin' happened the way you promised. You said I'd run this place someday, well I ain't runnin' nothin'. You said Rachel would come around, well she ain't never come around, she's closed up and miserable and I can't stand it, knowin' that I am the thing that's makin' her that way.
[NED: You just goin' through a hard time now. You just got to have faith—]
RUDY: Faith! Faith! Open your eyes and look around. That girl can't hardly abide me. Look at how she looks at me. You are blind, you can't see that. Hell, I had to be crazy to listen to you. I know I ain't much to look at. And I may not be all that smart. But I'll tell you this much. If I ever have any children, I ain't never gonna do to them what you done to yours.

# Hanging Lord Haw-Haw
Jeffrey Hatcher

**Scene:** England 1930s

**Serio-comic**
William Joyce (20s–30s), a passionate young fascist.

Joyce has met his match in the beautiful young Margaret White, who shares his desire for Great Britain to join with Germany in an attempt to bring about a new world order. Here, Joyce proposes.

JOYCE: A few things you should know about me. I am the product of a Jesuit education. Every mass, I swung the censer with such vigor that the glowing incense was scattered down the aisle. I had a nun who said I would either do something very great in the world, or finish on the end of a rope. Sister Cassandra. One time, I was sent off the rugby field because, though I played with great vigor, I did not seem to know which side I was on. I am a patriot. In college my mates knew that by whistling the national anthem they could get me to leap out of my cot and stand to attention. I have read widely in languages, history, philosophy, psychology, economics, and the law. I like Wagner, hate the cinema, loathe the theater, but will go to Gilbert and Sullivan if pressed. I can play chess, but I do not strategize. As for the future, a gypsy read my palm once and said that my head line, though clear and sharp, was extremely short. I think she said my life-line was short as well. And I have a scar.
[MARGARET: I hadn't noticed.]
JOYCE: I think we should have tea together. In fact, would you consider marrying me?

# Heading West
Philip Goulding

**Scene:** A farm in New Hampshire, 1850

**Dramatic**
Edward (20–30), a young man grieving for his dead wife.

Edward and Lizzie risked everything when they left England for a better life in America. When Lizzie dies in childbirth, Edward can find no love in his heart for his infant daughter as he here reveals.

EDWARD: I can't seem to look at her, I dunno why. Whether it's I blame her somewhere dark inside myself or just cos I fear, as you say, that it'd be like looking at Lizzie herself . . . I don't know what it is, but I just can't seem to face her. Oh I know the child ain't to blame, I know that in my head, and I know she's part of Lizzie and part of me and so I should feel something . . . else from what I do, but I just can't. I thought I was a strong man George, but I been laid low by this and I can't seem to figure out the right way through. It's all just anger over why, and when we'd come so far, and it was only ever her as had the answers and now she's gone and I feel so bloomin useless and so lost and so alone . . .

# The Invention of Love
Tom Stoppard

**Scene:** England, 1936

**Dramatic**
A.E.H. (77), A. E. Housman; scholar and poet.

> Upon his death, AEH is ferried across the River Styx by Charon and is brought face-to-face with his younger self. A discussion of the love shared between comrades in arms leads A.E.H. to make the following observations about his own unrequited feelings for Moses Jackson, the man he loved for his entire life.

A.E.H.: To be the fastest runner, the strongest wrestler, the best at throwing the javelin—this was virtue when Horace in his dreams ran after Ligurinus across the Field of Mars, and Ligurinus didn't lose his virtue by being caught. Virtue was practical: The athletic field was named after the god of war. If only an army should be made up of lovers and their loves!—that's not me, that's Plato, or rather Phaedrus in the Master of Balliol's nimble translation: "although a mere handful, they would overcome the world, for each would rather die a thousand deaths than be seen by his beloved to abandon his post or throw away his arms, the veriest coward would be inspired by love." Oh, one can sneer— the sophistry of dirty old men ogling beautiful young ones; then as now, ideals become debased. But there was such an army, a hundred and fifty pairs of lovers, the Sacred Band of Theban youths, and they were never beaten till Greek liberty died for good at the battle of Chaeronea. At the end of that day, says Plutarch, the victorious Philip of Macedon went forth to view the slain, and when he came to that place where the three hundred fought and lay dead together, he wondered, and understanding that it was the band of lovers, he shed tears and said, whoever suspects baseness in anything these men did, let him perish.

[HOUSMAN: I would be such a friend to someone.]

A.E.H.: To dream of taking the sword in the breast, the bullet in the brain—

[HOUSMAN: I would.]

A.E.H.: —and wake up to find the world goes wretchedly on and you will die of age and not of pain.

[HOUSMAN: Well—]

A.E.H.: But lay down your life for your comrade—good lad!—lay it down like a doormat—

[HOUSMAN: Oh—!]

A.E.H.: Lay it down like a card on a card-table for a kind word and a smile—lay it down like a bottle of the best to drink when your damn fool life is all but done: any more laying-downs we can think of?—oh, above all—*above all*—lay down your life like a pack on the roadside though your days of march are numbered and end with the grave. Love will not be deflected from its mischief by being called comradeship or anything else.

# The Invention of Love
Tom Stoppard

**Scene:** England, 1936

**Dramatic**
   Oscar Wilde (40s), playwright and poet.

   Encountering A. E. Housman in the afterlife, Wilde takes a moment to contemplate the invention of love.

WILDE: Once, I bought a huge armful of lilies in Covent Garden to give to Miss Langtry, and as I waited to put them in a cab, a small boy said to me, "Oh, how rich you are!" . . . "Oh, how rich you are!" *(He weeps.)* Oh—forgive me. I'm somewhat the worse for—cake. I have tried to give it up, whenever I feel myself weakening I take a glass of cognac, often I don't eat cake for days at a time; but the Jubilee broke my will, I allowed myself a social éclair out of politeness to my guests, and remember nothing more until I woke up in a welter of patisseries. Oh—Bosie! *(He weeps.)* I have to go back to him, you know. Robbie will be furious but it can't be helped. The betrayal of one's friends is a bagatelle in the stakes of love, but the betrayal of oneself is lifelong regret. Bosie is what became of me. He is spoiled, vindictive, utterly selfish and not very talented, but these are merely the facts. The truth is he was Hyacinth when Apollo loved him, he is ivory and gold, from his red rose-leaf lips comes music that fills me with joy, he is the only one who understands me. "Even as a teething child throbs with ferment, so does the soul of him who gazes upon the boy's beauty; he can neither sleep at night nor keep still by day," and a lot more besides, but before Plato could describe love, the loved one had to be invented. We would never love anybody if we could see past our invention. Bosie is my creation, my poem. In the mirror of invention, love discovered itself. Then we saw what we had made—the piece of ice in the fist you cannot hold or let go. *(He weeps.)* You are kind to listen.

# The Judas Kiss
David Hare

**Scene:** London, 1895, and Italy, 1897

**Dramatic**
Oscar Wilde (40s), Irish playwright and poet.

Wilde has been found guilty of committing acts of "gross indecency" and has been given a choice of prison in England or exile. Here, the great playwright defends his decision to remain in England.

WILDE: So. They choose to offer me this opening. The whole world wants me to go.
[ROSS: Yes.]
WILDE: The world persists in thinking me shallow. They think me feckless. They consider me weak. Flee, and I hand them this ready opinion. Do you know I think I may have decided? *(He moves to the wine, resolved.)* Open my case, I beg you. I wish to sit here. I wish to read. I shall not run down this hole they have dug for me. I will not stoop to leave on all fours.
  *[(Ross puts the cases back on the bed in despair.)]*
Yes. I can run but I choose not to. Die of embarrassment in some hovel abroad? Admit to society they have driven me out? No, I will not give them that pleasure. I am going to do the single thing which will drive them to frenzied distraction: I am going to sit down and get on with my lunch. *(He sits rather clumsily down at the table and contemplates the meal in front of him.)* My mind is made up. Good. A book. Yes, a book, please, Robbie.
  *(Ross re-opens the case to get him a book. Wilde lifts his knife and fork, but for a moment they are suspended.)*
If I run now, my story is finished. For as long as I stay it is not at an end. I prefer my story unfinished. *(He turns and looks at Ross.)* Robbie, we shall not discuss it. I shall eat and the train will make

**45**

its own way. Do you hear? Do you hear that whistle? *(He lifts a hand to his ear and waits.)* Do you hear the wheels running away down the track? What is that? The train is departing. Do you sense the life we did not live? *(He starts to tuck happily into the lobster.)* This lobster's good.

# The Judas Kiss
David Hare

**Scene:** London, 1895, and Italy, 1897

**Dramatic**
Oscar Wilde (40s), Irish playwright and poet.

Several years later, Wilde lives in unhappy exile in Italy. When his closest friend suggests that his lover, Lord Alfred Douglas, or "Bosie" has deserted him, Wilde angrily tells him to mind his own business.

WILDE: What is the fatal human passion? What is the source of all sin on this earth? This propensity in all human beings to indulge in the improper rapture, the gratuitous pleasure of giving others advice. Yes, I had rather swim neck-deep in London's arterial sewer, I had rather give up my body to every diseased and indigent tramp in the street, than surrender to this abominable indulgence of telling other people what they should do.
*(Ross looks down, rebuked.)*
It is not kind. It is not kind of you, Robbie. Is there not some small part of us which is purely our own? Which is our soul? Which is our innermost being? And which we alone should control? You bombard me. It is not fair. In any civilized war unfortified places are respected. I knew what you thought. You did not need to tell me. You know full well: I have done what I did out of love.
*(Ross looks back at him, saying nothing.)*
Do not . . . do not seek to destroy me by laying out what you call the facts. It is cruel of you, Robbie, it is cruel when you do such a thing. I have acted out of love. I have defended this love which exists between us, the purest I have known in my life. More perfect, more vital, more telling, more various, richer, more vibrant, more sweet. The redeeming fact of my life. *(He turns and*

*looks at Ross.)* It is what I have left. It is what remains to me. All else has now been taken away. So you would now take even that from me. You would tell me I have been deceived and used in all this? Consider what you are saying. If the love between us is not as I think, then I shall have suffered to no purpose at all.

# Just Taking Up Space
Nancy Gall-Clayton

**Scene:** A room in a nursing home

**Dramatic**
Frank Owen (18), a juvenile offender whose future is in question.

When a policeman attempted to give Frank a citation for defacing public property, he resisted and the ensuing scuffle landed the well-meaning cop in a coma. The judge has ordered that Frank visit the comatose officer for one hour every day. As the weeks go by, Frank finds that he's able to tell the sleeping policeman terrible secrets about his unhappy childhood. Here Frank tells Officer Arnie about a doomed fishing trip.

FRANK: Let's see, I was telling you about my dad's birthday. I was nine or ten. It was about a year before my dad disappeared on us. I got every fishing pole out of the cellar and managed to get them down to the riverbank. I laid those poles out on the big rock where we fished and put little rocks on top of them so the poles wouldn't roll in. Then I just waited. Figured I'd have a mess of catfish for my dad. Surprise him real good, only, guess what? I fell asleep, and while I was asleep, a breeze came up, and those lines got a tangled up and not one of them with a fish on it!

I woke up with my dad standing over me hollering at me. He said my mother was worried about me and no one knew where I was and why did I think I could take other people's fishing poles. Then he tells me, "Franklin,"—he always called me "Franklin" when he was mad. "I'm going back for my birthday supper but you, *you* stay right here until you untangle those fishing lines!" And he left in a big huff. It was hard to do, real hard, and by the time I finished, my stomach was growling, my fingers were bleeding, and it was almost dark.

When I got home, no one was there. I found out later they'd gone to a movie. The cellar door was open, so I put the poles down there, and then I went in the kitchen. The cake plate was sitting next to the sink, but there wasn't a single piece left. I scraped some frosting off with my finger, but the dirt and the blood got mixed up with it. I had to spit it out. Then I went to bed in that empty house.

*(Pause.)*

I've never told anybody that story, not even Jenny. You know, I never even told my dad what I was trying to do, that it was all meant for a birthday gift.

# The Killer and the Comic
Rooster Mitchell

**Scene:** A remote cabin somewhere south of Buffalo, N.Y. The dead of winter

**Dramatic**
   Carl (32), a brutal serial killer with a book contract.

   Carl has retreated to this remote cabin to work on his book in which he describes his life as a killer. Here, he offers a comprehensive overview of his accomplishments and state of mind.

CARL: Solitude . . . from the outsider's prospective . . . For the most part quiet to a whisper . . . My dwelling, like my life, is empty desolate . . . Emphatically depressing to the stranger's eyes . . . One may envision the serene deathbed quarters of a hermit . . . But I know it better . . .
   *(Stops typing and looks up to the audience.)*
   . . . as the shocking palace of a madman.
   *(He slowly stands and saunters, with mad drive, to the front of the stage.)*
   I have little money and little possessions—and only a breath of my wits remain. Today, I've discovered I'm low on supplies and must soon scheme a jaunt to the store, which sits *(Points through the window.)* over the nearest hill, though far away. Not knowing if I'm wanted by the badge-wielding authorities always makes the trip to town a tense one. But I can only speculate, albeit blindly, that the murder of sweet Doris Webster was never solved. The fact that I sit here—dry, warm, and free, leads me to believe that the search might have concluded—or perhaps the wrong suspect is held in contempt for the bloody beheading of such a hauntingly innocent angel . . .

*(He takes a final drag off his cigarette. Puts it out on the floor, crushing it with his foot.)*

It's twenty chapters since I first called this *(Looks around.)* lost cabin home. Buried in the frost-covered winter woods, due south of Buffalo, I stumbled upon this cottage in the dead of December—nearly five years ago to this very day. I found this place a shambles—in my most preposterous state, cold sweating from the tumultuous events of the day. This place, the sight that it was; housed cobwebs which lined the ceiling, and hungry termites fed on the decaying walls. The floors covered my ankles with fist fulls of foreign dust. Cockroaches scurried until rats chased them away. I've since tidied the dwelling. Though hardly a picture you'd see on a magazine cover, I've made this shack livable. Mildly comfortable at best. I open the windows in the summer and occasionally, I'll make fires in the winter. I take such great pleasure in chopping firewood. Thick blocks of the tree's foundation appear impermeable to the naked hand, but melt effortlessly with the mere stroke of an axe blade. *(An odd grin.)* Oh—and the appliances abandoned maybe five or seven years ago, were left behind in working condition. A worn coffeemaker. A two-burner stove and a small refrigerator. Even the toilet works. But in the winter, the running water sometimes freezes, and I'm forced to defecate out back behind the cabin. This might offend most people. But I get used to the odor. *(A beat.)* When I'm alone, it is sickly quiet, indeed. But of late, my solitude has collided with intruders. A cross-country skier strayed from his companions or a misguided hunter wayward from his prey. They mysteriously fall upon my doorstep. And once they've seen me—my demonic and horrific twinges take over and I unravel into a most submissive routine. I ask them in. Invite them to stay the night. Make conversation. Offer a fresh cup of coffee, some whiskey, a cookie. Usually Chips Ahoy—as I recall, they enjoy the grandest shelf life. I'll ask them how they got lost and so on. *(Becoming meaner.)* I wait for the right moment and I grab my steely butcher knife. I walk to them and slit their necks. Not in front, but on the side; to stun them—much the way a mouse is conked on the head before fed to a snake, so he won't run wild in the cage. Then I tie them to a chair with old twine. And I stab them in the heart and kill them. I chop up their bodies. And I bury then out back. Twelve dismembered ill-fated visitors, in the form of mutilated stench-laden heads and bones, are stacked high in a fox hole out back. The hole, I might add, was dug in the midst of a nighttime drizzle with a potter's shovel, no more than five inches long, three inches wide. It's been an odd and uncharacteristically busy month for me and my horrific demons. I've killed two people these past two weeks alone. One, an ambitious oil surveyor in his 50s, who fought so hard, he broke two of my ribs. The other, a door-to-door bible salesman, whose four-wheel pickup truck slid off the icy roads near the upstate turnpike. I do revel in watching one suffer with his last breath. Once the myoclonic jerks subside; once the victim has muddled the final of his blood-curdling screams; once the gruesome ranting and raving and painful shrieks fade to an unintelligible murmur, I stuff their chip-chopped remains into the makeshift grave, and fill it to the earth's surface with fresh dirt. Only then, can I resume my solitude.

*(He walks back to the desk, lights up another cigarette. Pours himself a slug of whiskey, slams it down. Sits on the desk.)*

My time alone is not completely encompassed with despair. I do cherish my fond memories of Doris Webster. She was, after all, my sexual awakening. With her subtle, blue eyes and her soft, baby-white skin. Chiseled cheekbones that cried to be caressed. *(Standing, moving about.)* Her shiny, golden hair, like streaming sheets of crystal clear rainfall. Her breasts were hard and round and her stomach was firm—sailing to her delicious paradise. Doris smelled and tasted like the world's most wonderful candy. Living . . . breathing . . . vivacious candy. *(A beat.)* But now she's nothing more than a tragic photograph imbedded in my mind. Was she the most vivid because she was my first love —or my first victim? *(A sinister laugh.)* I still cannot know for certain, so I don't interrogate the irony. But I do know this: No thought of Doris Webster, happy or sad, concludes without the hostile images of her hellish devastation. *(Beginning to get aroused by this.)* And now . . . my love for Doris can only be mirrored by the explicit action that ended her existence. I speak of Murder! *(Sinister.)* Unadulterated MURDER! Yes. I now lust for murder! *(More sinister.)* An insane passion swirls in my gut with the mention of the word. That word, murder! Sweet like nectar! Twisting a gleaming knife into the pit of a stomach! Flipping the blade like a joystick through the abdomen and RIPPING away the tender flesh! Slicing intestines into severed strings of grotesque matter, grotesque nothingness. *(Slows down.)* Creating the uncompromising vat— of human destruction.

*(Carl walks back to the typewriter. Sits, begins talking and typing again.)*

I prefer . . . knives to guns. Death by . . . .firearm is a paradox . . . A hasty neglect to the essence of . . . murder . . . Murder should be slow, tortuous. Mad, cruel, and villainous . . . After all . . . a dribbling infant . . . could pull a trigger . . . The great killers are desperate men . . . painstakingly loyal . . . to their insanity . . . I, too, am loyal . . . to mine.

# The Killer and the Comic
Rooster Mitchell

**Scene:** A remote cabin somewhere south of Buffalo, N.Y. The dead of winter

**Serio-comic**
   Barney (62), a comedian who never made it, a Catskills wannabe.

   Barney's car has suffered a flat during a blizzard. Here, he tells his tale of woe to Carl, in whose cabin he's found temporary refuge.

BARNEY: So get this. Me and Mort. We're flying down Route 22. *(Roams as Carl watches, wordless.)* I'm talkin' 50 miles an hour. So I says, Mort. For Christ sake, slow down. Nah, he says. I run these roads for years. I know every turn, every twig, every bump from here to Buffalo. So he doesn't slow down. Not even a kilometer per second. I don't know metric from gonorrhea, but I know we're near Canada. Trust me on this one.
   *(Carl cannot believe this joker, but he doesn't say anything. He just scopes his prey.)*
   So I says, Mort. You schmuck. You lymph node on the ass of a gibbon. There's enough ice on this fakakta road to make Ethiopia a skating rink. He still doesn't slow down. All of a sudden, a fog blankets the street and he loses all visibility. He cuts it to the left, to the right. He makes every move but the hokey-pokey and the next thing you know, we're two balding Jews careening off the road in a rented Lexus. *(Gets closer to Carl.)* Which, by the way, ain't a bad car. Mort's got a brother in Albany that sets him up. Personally, I can't stand the fat bastard. Not Mort, his brother. Where was I? Oh yeah. *(Walks away again.)* So we fly off the road into a guardrail. We get a flat. I says, Mort. Goddamit. Look what you've done. We got two shows tomorrow

night at the Buffalo Sheraton. And instead of goin' through the act, we gota' play Jeremiah Szedrate and Grizzly Schmuck in some backwoods, blizzard filled, bullshit landfill. So I says, I'm gonna' call for help. You're the putz that got us into this mess, so y*ou* change the fakakta tire. I pointed to your cabin and said meet me at Abe Lincoln's wooden wet dream in twenty minutes. So tell me. You gota' phone?

# Listening To Insomnia
Amy Beth Arkawy

**Scene:** A cell on Death Row, the night before the big day

**Dramatic**
#90600 (20–40) s man who may or may not be a killer contemplating his last day on earth.

#90600: That sound. That sound's what I'll miss. *(Pause, maybe a laugh.)* Really. Twelve years of CLANK, CLANIK, CLANK! Loud . . . Hollow . . . Everlasting. It sort of seeps into your pores, clogs up your soul . . . if you got one. But tomorrow at six PM I'm out of here. Gone like the wind. Free as a friggin' bird. So don't go feeling sorry for me. Christ, anything but that. Not like those pro-choice, anti-death do-gooding liberal losers with their protests and sorry posters and last-minute calls to the governor. "Save him." "Spare him." From what? CLANK, CLANK, CLANK? Don't be wasting your tears. Four thirty tomorrow I'm eating lobster and curly fries . . . the hot and spicy kind . . . I'll risk indigestion. And a Yoo-hoo, a Budweiser and a HI C. And two Hershey bars, the big ones with almonds. No point in pulling a Karla Faye Tucker . . . that stupid Texas bitch . . . her last supper was a friggin' salad and a Diet Pepsi. What's she counting calories for? I don't know what's over there, but I sure as hell don't think St. Peter, or whoever's doing the counting . . . up or down . . . is dressed like some freakin' Richard Simmons with a calculator.
   *(Beat.)*
   For the record, I got no one left to say good-bye to. Not even my mama, who died like she lived, stuck to a stool down at The Glory Bar, downing daiquiris by the gallon. The old bitch visited me but one time—before I was convicted when she was still tellin' people her "baby boy" couldn't have done such a thing. She came to see me up at County—brought me long john underwear, a crappy, used Walkman with a freakin' Gordon Lightfoot

tape stuck inside and a mess of paperback books—mostly Stephen King and Deepak Chopra. Then after that jury did their duty, she just went back to the bar. She couldn't make the trip—it was "too far and too depressing." Oh, for a while she'd send letters always filled with talk of some guy she knew who knew this big shot, big time New York lawyer who could handle the appeal "all the way to the Supreme Court." But the guy never showed. I kept getting the court-appointed nimrods with the bad suits who just barely passed the bar exam on the fifth try. And finally her liver gave out and she passed on three years, four months and two days, before her "baby boy."

In prison doing time means counting it—year by year, day by day, hour by hour.

Okay. Did I do it? That's what you want to know, right? It's okay, that's what they all want to know—the lawyers, the psychiatrists, the reporters, even the schoolgirls who read *Prison Pen Pal Monthly* and still write after their mothers find out. Did I rape and strangle four teenage girls behind the junior high school and then try to burn them beyond recognition in a bonfire started by copies of *Curious George* and *The Grapes of Wrath?*

That's the one question I can't . . . no the one question I WON'T answer. Why should I? The jury did it for me . . . for them. Let it be on those twelve heads. Let them spend sleepless nights wondering if those unidentified smudged fingerprints meant anything . . . if the eyewitness was really a drunk half-blind attention-seeking nut job whose brother-in-law owed me over five hundred dollars for two perfectly good, slightly illegal VCRs? . . . . If science will find a way to dispute the indisputable DNA evidence, in say, twenty years.

By then it will be too late. For them. Not for me. Me—I'll be free. Free as a friggin' bird.

# Louis Slotin Sonata
Paul Mullin

**Scene:** Los Alamos, New Mexico, 1946

**Dramatic**
>Louis Slotin (30s), chief bomb-builder at Los Alamos hospitalized for a lethal dose of radiation obtained during a prompt burst from a plutonium bomb core.
>
>Following the tragic accident, Louis can only lie in a hospital bed and await the inevitable. Here, he dreams he is a black soldier taking a part in the D-Day invasion of Normandy.

DREAMER A: It's June the 6th, 1944.
DREAMER B: I'm in an amphibious landing craft headed straight for Omaha Beach.
DREAMER A: Normandy.
SLOTIN: The time is come. As I look around at the other soldiers puking up their last rations as the LC bounces across the channel's heavy chop I realize a strange thing:
BLACK SOLDIER: I am a black man.
SLOTIN: I have always been black.
DREAMER A: From Arkansas maybe, or the Carolinas.
DREAMER B: I am the only Negro on this boat.
BLACK SOLDIER: Hell, I'm the only Negro in this entire invasion.
DREAMER A: And even with the shells sending up columns of sea and spray all around us.
DREAMER B: And even with the shore looming closer and closer, and the thrill and terror pumping so thick I can taste it, I have to laugh.
SLOTIN: Because I realize there's been some mistake:
BIACK SOLDIER: This ain't my war.
DREAMER A: The boat hits the beach.

DREAMER B: We can hear the bullets clanging on the other side of the steel landing ramp.

DREAMER A: And then down it goes.

DREAMER B: And we can see machine-gun fire churning the water in front of us to a wall of froth.

BLACK SOLDIER: Ain't nobody stepping into that. But when I turn round, I see the Navy skipper's pointing his sidearm Colt at us from the other side. So what do we do but go? White boys falling all around me. Some cut to pieces by the guns, some just drowning under their gear. But I move forward. The Kraut bullets just won't hit me. This ain't my war.

    I got me a Browning Automatic Rifle, a big ol' bloody BAR and I start pumping her good into anything the moves up on them cliffs. And then I'm up the cliffs. I leave all them white boys behind dying and such down on the beach. Ain't got time for that. Ain't my war. Every lousy Kraut beady blue-eyed bastard I see, I just jerk back on my BAR and pump some lead in their face. "Damn, Fritz. You sorry now, ain't ya? Should a thought a that sooner, huh? Now get down in hell where you belong."

DREAMER A: And then I'm running.

DREAMER B: Running ahead.

BLACK SOLDIER: I ain't got time for this. This ain't my war.

SLOTIN: I run past Paris.

BLACK SOLDIER: Sorry, Ladies. Much as I'd like, ain't no time for that now.

DREAMER A: I run forward.

SLOTIN: Past the Maginot line.

DREAMER B: Into Germany.

BLACK SOLDIER: And I kill the Krauts when I see 'em, but I ain't wasting no time neither.

DREAMER A: I'm running.

DREAMER B: Past Berlin.

SLOTIN: Past Hitler.

BLACK SOLDIER: Ain't got time for that lousy little shit-ass now. Let 'em eat his own lead.

DREAMER A: I'm running.

DREAMER B: I'm into Poland now.

DREAMER A: And then I'm there.

SLOTIN: Auschwitz.

BLACK SOLDIER: And damned if it don't look just like *Gone With The Wind*. Big ol' plantation with a big ol' pearly white house with big ol' columns. And who you think's sitting up on that porch, just sipping on a julep but the Doctor himself.

SLOTIN: Mengele.

BLACK SOLDIER: All right. Now we got somebody worth killing. I stroll on up them front steps drop my bar from my shoulder, and get set to shoot, only the gun ain't a gun. Just a damned stick.

DREAMER A: A yardstick.

DREAMER B: A slide rule the size of a yardstick.

DREAMER A: It's hard to say.

SLOTIN: At any rate, Mengele smiles. He gets up, and from his vest pocket draws a very small knife.

DREAMER A: A scalpel.

BLACK SOLDIER: And cuts me open.

SLOTIN: To find the smallish Canadian Jew inside.

BLACK SOLDIER & SLOTIN: Louis.

BLACK SOLDIER: And right then and there it dawns on me.

DREAMER A & DREAMER B: *(Together.)* We got trouble.

# Louis Slotin Sonata
Paul Mullin

**Scene:** Los Alamos, New Mexico, 1946

**Dramatic**
Louis Slotin (30s), chief bomb-builder at Los Alamos hospitalized for a lethal dose of radiation obtained during a prompt burst from a plutonium bomb core.

When Philip Morrison, head of the Los Alamos lab, visits Slotin in the hospital, the once vibrant young scientist reveals his fears for the future of a world containing nuclear weapons being handled by humans who are naturally prone to make mistakes.

SLOTIN: I was reading your testimony before the Senate special committee on Atomic Energy.
[MORRISON: Louie, why—]
SLOTIN: It's incredible. You're so gifted in so many ways. To be able to get up in front of those people and tell the truth like you did.
[MORRISON: Trust me, it wasn't—]
SLOTIN: Listen to what you said about Nagasaki and Hiroshima: "Many literally crawled out of the wrecks of their homes relatively uninjured. But they died anyway. They died from radiation that affects the blood-forming tissues in the bone marrow. The blood does not coagulate, but oozes in many spots through the unbroken skin, and internally seeps into the cavities of the body. The white corpuscles which fight infection disappear. Infection prospers and the patient dies, usually two or three weeks after the exposure.
[MORRISON: Why are you doing this, Louie? Why can't you—]
SLOTIN: Just die? I don't want to just die. And listen to this in your conclusion: "It goes without saying that, like most of the scientists

of the project, I am completely convinced that another war cannot be allowed. We have a chance to build a working peace on the novelty and terror of the atomic bomb." . . . Novelty and ter ror. Brilliant. But what happens when—and maybe this is what I'm getting at—what happens when the novelty of the terror wears off and people get cavalier . . . sloppy? Like me?

[MORRISON: Louie—]

SLOTIN: Jesus Christ, Phil. I don't wanna be a metaphor.

[MORRISON: You're not a metaphor, Louie. You're a human being.]

SLOTIN: Yeah, but for how long? . . . Maybe the best I can hope for is to be a metaphor. I certainly don't want to be a damned hero or martyr. I wish . . . no one would remember me at all. I hope one day not a soul will remember my name.

[MORRISON: Louie . . . ]

SLOTIN: No, I'm serious. Jesus Christ, Phil, think of it! Of all the things a man might be remembered for, I'll be remembered for my arrogance and my stupidity. Was I really that bad, Phil, that I should deserve such a fate?

[MORRISON: No.]

*(Pause.)*

SLOTIN: Rhetorical question, ya dope.

# Louis Slotin Sonata
Paul Mullin

**Scene:** Los Alamos, New Mexico, 1946

**Dramatic**
　Israel Slotin (60s), Louis's father.

　The army would like to perform an autopsy on Louis so to better understand how to combat radiation poisoning. When the request is made of Israel, he makes the following difficult decision.

ISRAEL SLOTIN: Dr. Hempelmann. . . shhh. . . Have some whiskey.
　*(Pause.)*
　My son, such a brilliant boy. Always working. Always studying, thinking, tinkering, figuring. Did you know that when Louie's high school pals would come over, he'd have his little brother Sammy play bridge with them while he went and studied. He liked to sit and read in the gazebo I built in the backyard. When he got his Ph.D. degree in London, of course I told everyone I knew. "My son's a doctor," I said. And they'd say, "Oh, a doctor?! So what kind of doctor is he?" And I would reach out for a light switch on the wall and turn it on and off. And I would say, "Do you know where the light went? . . . No? . . . You don't know. I don't know. But my son Louis, he knows. *That's* the kind of doctor he is." A scientist. So smart. So much smarter than any of us. Too smart maybe. Ah, who knows? But he wants this thing . . . so you say.
[MORRISON: Mr. Slotin . . . He—]
ISRAEL SLOTIN: You said he wants it. Right?
[MORRISON: Yes.]
ISRAEL SLOTIN: But it's my decision.
*(Pause.)*
[MORRISON: Yes.]

ISRAEL SLOTIN: Good thing you're a scientist, Phil. You'd make a lousy businessman. One thing I'll say for us Jews. We know how to prevaricate. You know what this means? Prevaricate? What am I saying? Of course you know what it means: you're a learned man. Now Jesus, there was a Jew. Needless to say and I mean no offense, but I don't think he was the son of god any more than I am, but . . . he was a Jew for sure. He talked like a Jew . . . lotsa times. I know. Believe it or not I've read the stories. Like when somebody tried to trick him up about paying taxes to the Romans he took a look at the coin with Caesar's face on it and said, "Render unto Caesar that which is Caesar's and render unto God that which is God's." It's a very Jewish solution. You say my son would want this, because he was a scientist, I imagine, and what is this but more science. Right? I say . . . true enough . . . My son gave himself to this world . . . this world of science and bombs and accidents and autopsies. I say render unto Caesar that which is Caesar's. So do your autopsy. Do it quickly. But I don't want you to touch the face or any part of the head. Is this understood?
[HEMPELMANN: Well . . . ]
[MORRISON: Yes.]
[HEMPELMANN: All right. Thank you, Mr. Slotin.]
ISRAEL SLOTIN: Don't thank me. Drink your whiskey. I'm going to bed.

# The Martyrdom of Washington Booth
Jeni Mahoney

**Scene:** The rural northwest

**Dramatic**
   Mobu (30s), a Tutsi terrorist.

   Mobu has transported a deadly virus to the U.S.A. at the bequest of Washington Booth, a self-proclaimed patriot who intends to use the virus to kill Jews, homosexuals, abortionists, et al. in the name of God. Here, Mobu poses an important question regarding God's motivation.

MOBU: My brother thought he was divining God's will—that all men should love each other. But it is not natural. We know it is not natural—not because God said so—but because it has never NEVER worked. Our only choice is to accept our own nature and rid ourselves of the thing that makes us angry. The thing we cannot control. The thing that is different. In this God is irrelevant. When the Hutus were killing my people, they ran to the churches for safety and do you know what the priests told them? "God is through with you now. Sit in the church, they will come and kill you soon." And they believed that it must be true because otherwise God would not have permitted it to happen. I think God must have looked on in amusement at this spectacle. These people were defeated—not by God—but by an incredible suppression of their own biological nature. It is the nature of every living cell to struggle for life. Yet these people sat patiently as ducks and waited to be destroyed. I understood then that for all this talk of Allah—God's will—the real enemy is our own nature, that can so casually betray us. What side God is on? Tell me.

# The Most Fabulous Story Ever Told
Paul Rudnick

**Scene:** Here and now

**Comedic**
Trey Pomfret (30s), a pissed-off, gay man dressed as Santa Claus.

Trey was inspired by his friend's renewed interest in the Bible to volunteer as Santa on Christmas Eve in a homeless center. Here, he returns from his disastrous appearance in need of spiritual counseling and a soft drink.

TREY: *(To Adam.)* I am so pissed at you!
[ADAM: At me? Why?]
TREY: Because of all this Bible business!
[CHERYL: Bible?]
TREY: I am an over-bred, over-educated WASP from Connecticut, so I've always thought of God as, you know—an ancestor. But lately Adam's been going on, about miracles, and his little Bible pageant, so I thought, well, I'll try. *(Noticing Cheryl's poinsettia plant.)* Oh look, it's a poinsettia—the gift that won't die. So I don this ensemble and I volunteer, on Christmas Eve, at the local homeless shelter. Where I have just allowed countless heart-breakingly innocent, bright-eyed homeless children to sit on my lap. "Ho, ho, ho, and what would you like for Christmas, little Simbali, or Jamal, or Tylenol?" *(Going over to shake Cheryl's hand.)* I can make these jokes because my name is Trey and my brothers are named Shreve and Stone, so who am I to talk? And little Advil says, "Santa, whassup? Is you a faggot?"
[CHERYL: No!]
[ADAM: What did you do?]

TREY: Well, I took a deep breath, and I said, "Why yes I am, little Midol. And the North Pole is for everyone, gay and straight."
[ADAM: That's perfect.]
[STEVE: And what happened?]
TREY: Armageddon. The child's hard-working, down-on-her-luck single parent grabs the child off my lap and screams, "Get away, cocksucker!" To which I reply, "But darling, look what I've brought for you—Christmas crack." And finally the director of the shelter says that maybe it's best if *I* leave! So I come here, and my question for you, Adam, is this—what the fuck is God thinking?

# New York Actor
John Guare

**Scene:** A theater bar in Manhattan—Joe Allen's to be precise

**Serio Comic**
  Craig (30–40), an actor recently returned to New York from L.A.

  Here, Craig explains why he decided to call it quits in L.A.

CRAIG: It's like what Laurence Olivier said, "If acting decides to embrace you and take you to its heart, it will hurl you up there among the gods. It will change your wooden clogs over night and replace them with glass slippers." I'm not saying I'm Sir Larry—
[EILEEN, BARRY and NAT: No no no.]
CRAIG: But I'm thrilled to be back in New York. Out there I was ready to kill myself. That's what scared me. I finally got the courage to do it.
[NAT: Kill yourself?]
CRAIG: Terminal likeability. The L.A. disease. Any time you read a freeway fatality, know it's an L.A. actor who crashed his Volvo into an overpass, sick of being likeable. That's—that's what happened to me.
[EILEEN: No!]
CRAIG: I tried to crash my new Volvo into a rail guard on the freeway. I pulled over to the side of the road—
[NAT: Where?]
CRAIG: Out by Valencia. Asthmatic. Gasping for breath. Sweating. Freezing. My series was cancelled. Going through yet another pilot season. No pilot. My daughter comes to me and says, "Daddy, I want breast implants." I said, "Francesca, you're six years old." This L.A. child looks up to me and says, "I don't give a shit. I want them and I want them now." What kind of values are these? My boy Milo is always in his mother's sewing kit. Playing with needles. We can't tell if he's going to be a junkie or

a costume designer. What strangers am I raising? Katinka and I gave 'Cesca a gift certificate for some work on her nose which shut her up but only for a while and now she's here getting her head on—I hope. Katinka and I are frightened. Where was I headed? *Lawyer* cancelled. I went up for another series. This time the friend of the best friend. The beginning of the downward spiral. I aimed my Volvo right into the rail guard.
[NAT: Hey, you're safe. You're here.]
CRAIG: And then the call came.
[EILEEN: I'm so glad you're back. And alive. Bravo.]
[NAT: You can use that. The asthma. The freezing.]
[BARRY: I was up for a Volvo commercial. Voice-over.]
CRAIG: The difference between being an L.A. actor and a New York actor is in L.A. you don't ever dare be tuned out of somebody's living room. Never be unpleasant or complicated. But a New York actor is fearsome. A New York actor changes his soul. A New York actor has a soul to change. Christ, listen to me. I'm alive! Being what God meant me to be!

# No One Talks to the Mailman
Christopher Wall

**Scene:** Will's childhood home in the woods outside town

**Dramatic**
Will (30), a man haunted by memories of a violent childhood.

His father's abuse has driven Will quite literally into his mother's arms, resulting in an illicit sexual relationship. Here, an older Will recalls the moment after which there was no turning back for either of them.

WILL: I don't remember the stairs. The first step into the basement. Or how we ended up. In a corner. Between the boxes. Ma looked at me. A halo of dust. Tangled hair. As if to say something. Then turned and picked up a box. Moved it, left to right. No words. A sigh. Clenched teeth. Left to right. She struggled. Something heavy. My hands went out. And we stood there. Between everything. Holding a stupid piece of cardboard. That was my chance. I see that now. There were a million ways out. I could drop it.
*(He mimes dropping a box.)*
Kick it.
*(He kicks it.)*
Scream.
*(He screams.)*
Tell a joke. God. The possibilities! But I took it from her, instead. Started a pile. She lifted another. We fell in together. An assembly line. Left to right.
*(Pause.)*
In between the activity, I peered over my shoulder for this taller, more-together woman. Hoping to catch, in the corner of my eye—And she turned, looking for this scrawny kid who never screwed up. I turned. She turned. I turned. And thought—Christ.

Here we are in the basement, looking for ghosts. Things that passed out of the world.

*(He laughs.)*

She would've liked that. If I'd told her.

*(Lights up on Terra in the kitchen, waiting for him. Will senses her, though he still looks out to the audience.)*

I always end up here. In between. I see things that shouldn't exist. People who never met. Moments a decade apart. Faces swirling around. I used to be able to keep them apart. It was easy. I could leave. Close my eyes.

*(He closes his eyes.)*

Pretend not to hear.

*(From the kitchen.)*

[TERRA: Will?]

WILL: Pretend.

[TERRA: Will?]

WILL: Keep the past past. The present present. Everything in its place. But somewhere. In between. It all stopped working.

# No One Talks to the Mailman

Christopher Wall

**Scene:** Will's childhood home in the woods outside town

> Will has fallen in love with Terra, who is pregnant with his child.
>
> Here, Will shares a memory of meeting Terra for the first time.

WILL: So I walk into the restaurant. Sea Coast Tavern. Order the lunch special. And ask the waitress, Terra, to leave with me. And she does. She's in the parking lot five minutes after she got off. I couldn't believe it. You should've seen me strutting around. Like some kind of Romeo.
*(Pause.)*
She didn't mention that her bags were already packed. That she'd crashed in this apartment three years, everything balled up in a suitcase. And had to get away. But it didn't matter if she told me or not. Cause what came after was real. And wonderful. Even the dumb stuff. Driving the back roads. My arm around her. Head on my shoulder. Right—Right here.
*(He touches his shoulder for a moment, lost in thought.)*
I had her body. Next to mine. Her hair on my neck. In the. goddamned truck. That's real. That doesn't go away. The rest of this is stories we tell each other. To pass the time. *(Beat.)* You can't hold a story.

# Perfect World
Linda Stockham

**Scene:** A Manhattan condo, New Year's Eve, 1993

**Dramatic**
  Denny Cryer (35), HIV positive, emotionally damaged.

  Denny has contracted HIV while in prison in the South China Sea. He blames his plight on his sister, Rosalind, a successful Broadway actress, who never responded to any of his letters begging for help. Here, he pays a visit to his estranged sister on New Year's Eve and reveals his intention to kill himself.

DENNY: I got something to say—something very, very important.
  *(There is something very cold in the way he says this. Kenneth nods to Sunny to take a seat next to Ruby. She does so.)*
  You're all full of *little red ants*—none of you got no idea what you're talking about.
  *(He gives out one of his grisly, unnerving laughs.)*
  You all have been so eager on knowing what I was doing in the South China Sea, haven't you? I was in prison. Well—a prison of a sort. It was more like a *goddamn* concentration camp.
[CORNEL: Why?]
DENNY: Gambling debts.
  *(Turns on Rosalind.)*
  I wouldn't have been there if you'd sent me the money I asked for. But you never even wrote back—didn't even ask why I wanted the money. I made a couple of bad calls and got kicked out of baseball. It was when I was coaching in Taiwan. I got out of Taiwan—first plane out of Taipei. It went to Jakarta—but these Chinese guys had pretty good connections down there. Next thing I know, I'm in some kind of island *stockade!*
  *(He looks around, his eyes darting about the room.)*

There were *pirates* in this camp. *Pirates!* That's what they said they were—but they was *filthy maniacs!* They beat me up something terrible, then raped me. For a long time, one of 'em *used* me over and over. Then, when he got tired of me, another one took me over—I just kept being passed around. I—I got AIDS. Why keep a dead man in prison? Why feed a dying man? They let me out with a one-way ticket to the U.S.A. Said I'd done my time. They put me on a boat to—some place on the west coast of the Philippines.
[CORNEL: Manila?]
DENNY: No—Maybe it was somewhere else. I was in a hospital . . .
[EDNA: On Taiwan? You said you flew back from Taipei?]
DENNY: *(To Rosalind.)* You didn't even write back, *rat-face*—
   *(Rebecca steps angrily forward.)*
[REBECCA: I told you not to call Mom that—]
   *(Denny suddenly grabs Rebecca around the neck. Kenneth moves forward but Denny pulls a revolver from under his sweat shirt. He waves it toward Kenneth.)*
DENNY: Back, Mr. Lawyer.
[ROSALIND: *(Appalled and frightened.)* Denny, what are you doing? Don't hurt her—]
DENNY: Scared, *rat-face*? Good, cause I've been scared for so long. *(Crying out.)* Now—I just want to go home. To be buried, *rat-face*. To be buried in the family plot. But when I came here tonight, I wasn't sure what to do. But the *sacrificial* lambs—They make a lot of sacrifices to spirits and gods over in Asia. They sacrifice all kinds of things—
   *(Crying out, he puts the barrel of the revolver to Rebecca's head.)*
God—I don't want to die alone!

# The Power of Love
Sebastian Michael

**Scene:** Amsterdam and London

**Dramatic**
 Eugen (30s), a gay filmmaker.

 While on a working holiday in Holland, Eugen tells his partner about a time when he mistakenly had cyber sex with a thirteen-year-old.

EUGEN: I had the shock of my life
it was a secure adult zone how he got in there i don't know
and i just didn't realize
i thought his spelling was a bit erratic but
you know
some people can't spell for toffee
it doesn't make them kids
[TENDER: and did you stay in touch]
EUGEN: no
no
i did talk to him for about an hour afterwards on the net
trying to reassure him and
trying essentially to make sure he didn't feel awful about what he'd done
you've never seen anyone so
well
so indoctrinated i suppose: this kid tells me that gay people burn in hell
because that's what his parish priest told him
i mean do you see a millennium racing toward us?
that man must be in a century all of his own
now i've just made him have what was probably his first shared sexual

experience
on the net
what does that mean for him
does it mean *he* is going to burn in hell?

these people have no idea what kind of trauma they're setting their kids up for
with all that
guilt

but no
i didn't stay in touch with him
i didn't think it would be such a great idea

# The Power of Love
Sebastian Michael

**Scene:** Amsterdam and London

**Serio-comic**
   Eugen (30s), a gay filmmaker.

   Following a night of moderate debauchery Amsterdam-style, Eugen finds himself in the mood to make philosophical observations about human brainpower vs. human accomplishments.

EUGEN: you know that feeling when somebody calls you and you have a chat and before you hang up you do the "must-stay-in-touch" routine and just as you're about to ask them if they've got your phone number you think: hang on: i'm utilizing less of my brainpower here than my maker had probably had in mind
[TENDER: yes]
EUGEN: you do
[TENDER: not as such but i can imagine it
why]
EUGEN: do you ever just think out loud to yourself
[TENDER: not as often as you do]
EUGEN: i think it's crazy
[TENDER: asking somebody who's just called you whether they've got your telephone number]
EUGEN: no that's just absent-minded
what's genuinely crazy is that we've allowed ourselves to advance this far: michelangelo, da vinci, einstein, mozart: the usual suspects—now that's got to be the best constructed denouement in film history ever: the way he just reads it all off the board the way he just—we've come to *stephen hawking* while still only employing on average between five and ten percent of our brain power and if you watch the jerry springer show for instance or rikki lake

and you see the type of person who goes on there and grunts at somebody sitting two or three chairs removed from them about why they took their best friend's boyfriend's car without asking and are now pregnant by him though he's since had a sex change and wants to carry the kid herself, you realize that these people actually possess a working vocabulary of fifty-eight words, no more than that, and you think no: that's crazy they are a different species either that, or we're all conspiring in an exercise of human wastage on a scale so gargantuan that should we ever be brought to account—which i daresay we probably won't—it will be completely impossible to talk ourselves out of it. we will be standing there saying: yes i know. we had ninety percent of our kind operate at below ten percent of their potential at any given time. bummer really, arcadia was well within our grasp, we just, you know, couldn't be bothered, i guess lord strike me down i mean *strike me* down

# The Power of Love
Sebastian Michael

**Scene:** Amsterdam and London

**Dramatic**
   Eugen (30s), a gay filmmaker.

   Here, Eugen muses on unrequited love and growing old.

EUGEN: the man i'm in love with at the moment
also a man who doesn't love me, incidentally
at least i'm under the impression he doesn't love me
at least not as in "being in love with me"
he probably loves me well enough
at least he's gay so he could potentially love me
or say he could potentially fall in love with me
because of course he can love me whether he's gay or not
but he hasn't i don't think fallen in love with me
at least not as far as i'm aware
for reasons probably best known to him alone
otherwise i would have to handle knowing why he hasn't fallen in love with me
on top of the fact that he hasn't
which is depressing enough
well *he* says he's looking forward to being old
i never did
i never did look forward to being old
when i was eighteen i was looking forward to being twenty-three perhaps
it seemed a good step toward being adult
and being adult seemed a desirable goal at the time
as it happens i'm no more of an adult now aged thirty-three than i was then
at the age of eighteen
only a lot older

but i'm beginning
probably because paul
that's his name
got me onto the idea
i'm beginning to think that maybe i am looking forward to being old
i am beginning to think
yes
when i'm an old woman i want to wear purple with a red hat that doesn't go
imagine the release
from this obligation to be young and dynamic and handsome and fit
you could suddenly be
old and cantankerous
and set in your ways
and as long as you were quite eccentric
it would be almost
charming
as long as you've got your marbles and the body plays ball
more or less
so long as you're not actually falling apart: what a laugh
i mean you're laughing then aren't you
laughing
[TENDER: i didn't know you were in love]
EUGEN: oh yes
i am
i always am
always end up being
in love
but he lives twelve thousand miles away
in a place you've never even heard of called wollongong
south of sydney
so i suppose we're unlikely
to make a couple
in the immediate foreseeable future

# A Question of Mercy
David Rabe

**Scene:** Here and now

**Dramatic**
　　Dr. Chapman (50s-60s), a retired physician.

　　When Dr. Chapman is approached by a man who is dying of AIDS to help him end his life, he agrees. Here, he muses on his role as both savior and destroyer.

DR. CHAPMAN: An "angel" he calls me. An "angel." Well, maybe. *(He begins to change from his pajamas into a shirt, shoes, his suit.)* I know what he wants. It's a prayer, really. His prayer. Deliver him. Intercede. Give him the relief he needs. Fly to him, and with my bag of pharmaceutical tricks perform a miracle. Well, maybe. He calls to me, and I think, Is it really miracles that I bring? Well, maybe. Almost. Once I was to be his "instrument." Now I am his "angel." At first glance two very different things. And yet I'm wondering, Are they so different? Are they really so different? What both do, finally, is work the will of another. Some superior other? Both are in fact more or less useless until they're moved, until they are directed. So they're servants, really. Slaves, actually. And yet they share an appealing trait—a wondrous trait—one that I want, because of the way it will place me outside the compunctions and strictures holding me in. Such common human cares would have no meaning were I an instrument—no meaning were I an angel. *(He is in his suit now, facing out.)* As the one, I will be inanimate and mindless, and so completely unbothered by our moral fuss. As the other, as the angel, I will be supernatural. I will occupy a privileged realm beyond all recrimination.
　　*(He turns now and faces up center. Anthony is revealed*

*dressed in a suit. He stands near the couch and coffee table, holding a tray with water, pills, a glass.)*

DR. CHAPMAN: I will act from a place indifferent to reproach, no matter what I do, no matter how cataclysmic my deeds.

# A Question of Mercy
David Rabe

**Scene:** Here and now

**Dramatic**
Dr. Chapman (50s-60s), a retired physician.

Here, Dr. Chapman remembers the contributions of Ambroise Paré, the "father" of surgery.

DR. CHAPMAN: Ambroise Paré is often called the "father" of surgery. In the sixteenth century he accompanied the armies of France on their military campaigns, and in those killing fields he found an abundant resource for the education of his knife. Shattered limbs were plentiful. Wounds of every kind. Men maimed beyond hope and so docile before his desperate struggle to learn.
*(Music starts: the Pablo Casals recording of the 2nd Canon on the First Eight Bass Notes of the Aria Ground from Bach's "Goldberg" Variations once again. Variations 1, 2, 3, and 4.)*
DR. CHAPMAN: In the midst of the smoke and noise of battle, he entered a barn and found himself facing the bodies of four dead soldiers and three more who were still alive, their faces contorted with pain, their clothes still stinking and smoldering with the gunpowder that had exploded and burned them. In the pages of Paré's memoirs, he describes how there stood among them one old soldier. As Paré gazed at the wounded, writhing men with pity, the old soldier approached and asked whether there was any way to cure them. Paré shook his head no, and the old soldier turned and, in Paré's words, went up to the men and cut their throats "gently, efficiently, and without ill will." Paré cried out to the man that he was a villain. "No," said the man. "I pray God that if ever I come to be in that condition, someone will do the same for me." Villainy. Mercy. I see them now like two snakes coiled around a staff, their tangled shapes indistinguishable, their eyes fixed on each other.

# Rim of the Wheel
Daphne R. Hull

**Scene:** Baltimore, 1994

**Dramatic**
   Igor Vladimir Ilyich (23), a boy becoming a man, moody and thoughtful.

   Igor has recently immigrated to the U.S. from Russia. Here, he composes a letter to the girl he left behind.

IGOR: Dearest Alexia. My lost love. I have been in America for two months. I am terribly bored. I miss you. There are no jobs here, not what we thought would be waiting for us. Everywhere I go for work, I am questioned; not so much with words, but by the, eyes of my interviewers—my college does not seem to matter here. I am afraid I will have to attend an American college just to get a job for which I am qualified already. That would mean four more years from my life. Things would be so much easier in Russia. I would be holding you now. I would have a job to go to in the morning. We would have friends to drink with and talk with. And Baltimore—all the Russians emigrated to New York. Except us. I know we came here because we have family, which is nice, but I want my own life, my own friends. I will not find that here. I want to go home. To Russia. To you. My being here means so much to Mama, though, and I have to try.
   *(Alexia enters, stands beside him, rubs his face, shoulders, caresses and kisses him, etc.)*
   Mama—she cannot find a job either. Her being a journalist was a good thing at home, but here, journalists of course write in English, and Mama cannot write English. She may never learn to write it well enough to make money at it. She will probably end up cleaning some old person's house to make ends meet. But you know Mama, she is affected by nothing   she is convinced

that we will find our future here, and that the future is bright. Why am I not more like her? She lives for everything; right now I do not even know what I am living for. Yesterday I promised Mama I would give it a year. I am going to try my best to keep that promise.

*(Alexia exits, distressed.)*

I wait impatiently for your reply, my love, and until we meet again. All my love. Igor.

# Shoes
Sky Vogel

**Scene:** A small upscale shoe store

**Serio-comic**
   Dave (30s), a man lamenting his botched relationship with a woman he wanted to marry.

   Here, Dave describes his feelings of love to a woman he's just met in a shoe store.

DAVE: Let me ask you something. Do you ever wonder how it is that people get together? This day and age? Y'know? I mean . . . Look, just meeting people, *anyone* is hard enough. Meeting women—meeting *someone* of the opposite sex is going to be harder then, right? Now, add to that meeting someone of the opposite sex who you find attractive. Meeting someone of the opposite sex who you find attractive who finds *you* attractive. Meeting someone of the opposite sex, the attraction thing, and who's single! Unmarried. Not seeing anyone. Whatever. And of course, *you* gotta be single too! And then there's political affiliation, religion, which way you like the toilet paper to roll . . . So with all of this, I want to know how it is that anyone anywhere anytime is actually a couple! How *is* that? What are the odds?
   *(Pause.)*
   But you know what? It happened to me. Yeah. I won the lottery. Amazing. Don't ask me how. I don't remember any good deeds or signing my soul away. I just woke up one day and I . . . I felt—I feel—Am I making sense? It's like you're designed for each other. And life—my god, life is . . . Without even touching your chest you can actually feel your heart beating. And you're flying high. You're enjoying everything. Everything! Waiting for the subway. The godawful price for a candy bar. You're singing

along with TV commercials and saying hi to hot dog vendors. And it's the greatest feeling. The greatest . . . feeling.

   *(Pause.)*
[JACKIE: Dave, why did you come in here today?]
DAVE: I'm sorry. I really shouldn't . . .
[JACKIE: Dave?]
DAVE: It's just . . . a woman I like . . .
[JACKIE: Doesn't like you.]
DAVE: Doesn't like me.

# A Significant Betrayal
Le Wilhelm

**Scene:** Asa's home in the swamp

**Dramatic**
Asa (50s), reclusive, shut off from his family for thirty years.

Asa has been ostracized by his conservative family because he's gay. When his niece, Dorry, seeks him out and confesses that she is a lesbian, Asa reveals the incident that caused his exile involved her father.

ASA: She had a right to be angry.
*(There is a long silence.)*
[DORRY: How could you . . . you know?]
ASA: I didn't set out to . . . no one thought . . . everyone was young. Younger than you . . . your mother . . . I'm not sure why . . . it was here . . . the little field over there . . . the live oak . . . after it was all over . . . I always thought it would be struck by lightning . . . but it never has been . . . .it was them . . . and . . . what can I say . . . she was angry . . . who wouldn't be . . . you know it was over 30 years ago . . . I might have hoped the fires would dissipate by now . . . but . . . she still has that eternal flame of God's rage . . . at the time I didn't even know it was important . . . that took a while to set in . . . and in retrospect . . . in my musing out here at night when the fog comes in off the swamp and cocoons me . . . that's when I can think . . . I suppose from a distance it all seems very Biblical.
[DORRY: What?]
ASA: Nothing.
[DORRY: Biblical?]
ASA: The tree . . . and your mother's intended . . . it was my first . . . and she came upon it . . . and then ran back through the fields toward the house . . . the house where everyone was . . . I

think it was a birthday celebration for one of the old ones . . . something like that . . . back then they used to come to the old place . . . here to the swamp . . . and she ran back screaming . . . I tried to stop her. We both tried to stop her . . . but she was running and screaming toward the house and they ran out of the house . . . thinking there must be a rogue gator or something on the loose . . . maybe a wild boar'd come in out of the swamp . . . and we're running after her half dressed . . . and she's running as if a swarm of bees have settled in her hair . . . and then . . . there was quiet . . . and everything was changed forever . . . and God turned his back on me and took his angels away. Your mother's right to be angry . . . but if you get a chance let her know that there has been some small amount of punishment.

# A Significant Betrayal
Le Wilhelm

**Scene:** Asa's home in the swamp

**Dramatic**
    Asa (50s), reclusive, shut off from his family for thirty years.

    Here, a bitter yet philosophical Asa muses on life's tendency to betray.

ASA: Sometimes I think that's what life is.
[DORRY: Mmh.]
ASA: All life is.
[DORRY: *(Not really wanting to talk further.)* Is what?]
ASA: A series of betrayals.
[DORRY: That doesn't give a person much to look forward to.]
ASA: A series of betrayals. Surviving a series of betrayals until finally the body betrays the spirit and then you have the last of the betrayals. That's what your mother doesn't know . . . she just stayed here . . . she didn't go out . . . she doesn't understand that she doesn't hold the copyright on betrayals.
[DORRY: I think what happened would certainly make her a member of the club . . . considering the circumstances . . . and all . . . it would seem that she understands . . . ]
ASA: She doesn't understand anymore than what anyone can understand when you're young and . . . and neither can you . . . yes I betrayed her. And there was a time when I begged her to forgive me . . . did you know that? I don't suppose so. And I don't suppose she owes telling anyone any of it. But she said it was something that she couldn't forgive . . . and then the family they agreed with her. And they sent me away . . . I went up north . . . up around Tupelo . . . where Elvis was born . . . and stayed with cousins . . . who didn't know what had happened . . . the family wouldn't ever really let me be a part of it again . . . except for my

dad . . . who left me these forty acres . . . much to everyone else's chagrin, I might add . . . but them doing that . . . was understandable just like your mother . . . what she did was understandable . . . but what was not understandable was that all of a sudden my Master . . . had said depart from me . . . it was something I didn't know . . . that the Lord God Almighty . . . was not mine . . . had nothing to do with me . . . that I was an abomination to him . . . and I had been told that he loved all the children of the world . . . and now I was betrayed . . . and when I grew up and left . . . and . . . I was with people who considered God a crutch for the weak . . . but what they didn't understand is I needed that crutch . . . I was weak and I needed . . . I needed my angels . . . but if I believed what so many said I was part of a godless lot . . . and that's something . . . that's a betrayal too . . . when your God becomes your Judas. That's why I came back . . . Don't think I was miserable . . . I've lived all over this country . . . and I've had one night stands . . . more than I can count . . . and some meaningful relationships too . . . meaningful encounters can come in the strangest of disguises . . . but I came back because . . . because . . . I wanted to see if the angels were still here.

[DORRY: The angels?]

ASA: In antebetrayal times . . . by that I mean ante like in antebellum . . . in those times there were angels out here . . . I need them . . . Your momma and I, we used to go out where the swamp begins . . . where the alligators lie in wait . . . where the cypress hang heavy with spanish moss and the fog drips like tears from the eyes of all the once lovely people who have lost the battle to age and weep for beauty past. Your momma and I we'd come out here, when twilight was stealing across the lea and we'd look up at the moss and, and watch for angels . . . and we'd see them sometimes . . . their wings winnowing the air. Your momma, she'd take me when I was just a little thing . . . she's the one that taught me how to see them . . . we'd come down and see the moss move as the angels' wings . . . and then all that happened . . . and I never saw them . . . never saw the angels . . .

after your momma and I would go down here . . . mind you I was only six or seven at first . . . but I used to imagine the angels following us back up here and when I'd go to sleep at night I could feel them wrap their wings around me keeping me safe . . . everyone was so poor back then . . . your momma and the angels were the only comfort I had . . . and things were never the- same since . . . and when it all started going wrong . . . and haywire out there . . . I came back here looking for the angels.
[DORRY: Did you find them?]
ASA: I'm not sure . . . sometimes when twilight is stealing I think I might . . . but I'm not a little boy with his older sister now . . . it's not so easy now . . . it's not so easy to see them . . . to believe . . . but I desperately want them to be there.

# Sinatragate
Bob Jude Ferrante

**Scene:** Here and now

**Serio-comic**
   Bag Person (any age).

A street crazy who once dreamed of being a singer reminisces about a favorite conspiracy in which Frank Sinatra has actually been the president of the U.S. for fifty years.

*(Bagperson enters, singing to the tune of "Delta Dawn.")*
BAG PERSON: Delta Dawn, gots that flower you have on.
Could it be a faded nose from days gone by?
*(Speaks.)*
I'm confused, that's it. I used to be unconfused. To have certainty. Lots of. But now, certainty isn't something of which I can be certain. Certainty is for certain people. But not me. That's Truth. What is Truth? A cool breeze across your brain, one that makes it have nice little colored ripples, very attractive goes well with a dark suit. Suit. Suit.
*(Takes tongue out of his mouth and holds it for a moment.)*
Your tongue ever do this to ya? Man, I got serious tongue problems. A great effort to relate these universal truths, not that I'm trying to inspire guilt in you, you understand. O, listen, you get toe problems, that's nothing. Kidney—hey. What the heck. Leg, oh, yeah, yeah no big deal . . . Tummy . . . you'll live, but just wait until tongue problems start happening. Then you'll really have . . . I don't know, something like trouble. Exactly like trouble, so close to trouble it's virtually indistinguishable from trouble. Listen. I know courageous men—Sinatra!—had tongue problems. He sang "Strangers in the Night," his tongue would get a pang. He sang, "My Way," it would begin throbbing. He sang,

"New York New York," it almost fell out. But he sang on. What balls, what an amazing feat.

*(Pause.)*

Lived all these years and rarely have I seen something so feat . . . like . . . as the balls of his feat. I salute him. He was a God. Accomplished things this rock n' vole, forget it, the rock n' vole. Garbage. Frank could whip the pants off of *(Name a famous current rock star.)*. I mean it, Frank, *(Rock star.)*, in the ring, three rounds . . . *(Rock star's)* on his ass. Why? He's Frank! He did everything. He climbed buildings. People thought it was that guy with the suction cups. No! It was Sinatra. How do I know? I know Sinatra. We go back. I used to sing, and Frank used to encourage me. That's just the way he was. I was different then. Younger. I'm going to relate some serious truth now. You better sit. This is a big one. Sinatra, he was elected president fifteen times. You thought Roosevelt was president. There was no Roosevelt. That was Frank. Truman—Frank. Eisenhower—Frank. Kennedy—Frank! Johnson was a Sinatra character. And what an act was Nixon for Sinatra. A brilliant role. Then a humbling experience—Ford. He was absent-minded because he knew Kitty Kelley was—that bitch!—writing that goddamn book. Carter—man, did those teeth hurt Sinatra's tongue! But it was a harbinger of his craft, his greatness. A truly consummate performance—Reagan, old Rat-Pack buddy, begged, "Frankie, step in for the old Gipper." And Frankie delivered. A performance of such maturity, of subtle genius. From the heights of conservative bunkeroo to the depths of senility in just eight brief, brilliant years. Bushie was by comparison a vacation. And Clintie! You think Sinatra *likes* Mickey D's fries? He regrets he has but one gall bladder to give for his country. Amazing, to watch him age in office time and time again, as he gets young, old, thin, fat. Incredible makeup. So you wanna know who's gonna be the next president? Who's Sinatra doing now. But you gotta keep this under your hat, OK? Because if it ever got out, these truths I tell, it would be over. Finito. It would be . . . *Sinatragate!* Don't give me that "he's dead" shit. I don't wanna hear it. We got the C.I.A., we got the K.G.B., we got E.J.

Korvettes, you telling me anybody's ever dead? No way. I used to know him. I'll never forget what he said to me, that one day. He said, "Kid, don't ever stop singing. No matter what they say." That one time. And he threw me a buck.

*(Mimes flinging a silver dollar; suddenly he sounds like a much younger man.)*

A buck. Thanks Mr. Sinatra!

*(Taps his temple.)*

So I keep track. What do I look like to you, nothing, ha, yeah? *(Whispers.)* It's my secret identity. My moles, buried in the corridors of power, contact me and tell me his every move.

*(Makes a face.)*

They trust this face.

*(Makes different face.)*

Or maybe it's *this* face?

*(Beat.)*

Oy, I have to stop drinking. I'm going on the welcome wagon. I'm going to the Salvation Army. Yes I am, yes I am.

*(Exits, singing.)*

Smell that guy Shawn, take a shower or you're gone,
if I didn't plug my nose I think I'd die . . .

# Small Mercies
Heidi Decker

**Scene:** A small city park, outside an art museum

**Dramatic**
>Denis (30s), angry and frustrated by his inability to see the big picture.

>Here Denis paces in the park alone while revealing his delusional paranoia.

DENIS: I feel like I'm on the edge of something here . . . the threshold. Like in those movies where you see someone kind of dancing around, minding their own business, totally oblivious that they are standing on the edge of a cliff. Or maybe that's just cartoons. It's like there's this fog in my head and every now and then I see a glimpse of something . . . then it's gone. I thought I was . . . that I'd been, y'know, maybe chosen . . . but the visions they, they left me. Just up and *left*. Me. Alone. Maybe this is a test. Maybe this is hell. They come . . . they come to you . . . they come to you in visions, in revelations, in . . . in . . . in epiphanies and then, and then they leave you just as quick. They leave you behind. To remind you . . . that you, are nothing.
*(Pause, thoughtful, then.)*
I think God just has some kind of fucked up sense of humor. There's no proof that God isn't a freakin' maniac. Them . . . .they tease you. They come with all this flash . . . fanfare . . . beauty . . . and people say, others say, that's to show you what *could* be. What's coming. Give you hope.

Who says they're so generous? If that's true, why not now? Why not now, to me, to us, to all the fucked up people who need it? No, instead they let you glimpse it . . . for a second, this *blinding* second, and then they take it away. Why? What the fuck good does that do? I'll tell you why. Because they want to rub your face in it, that's why. Here's what you'll never have. See this? It's a fucking miracle and it's not yours. It's beauty it's peace, it's serenity, it's . . . ah ah ah, don't touch! Don't touch you lowly fucker. Do ya see it? Got a good look? Good. Because it's gone. Why? Because it's *not* yours. You *can't* have it, it *doesn't* belong to you. Not only that, but from now on *your* life is going to look twice as much like shit. *You* exist to give *us* something to do. What's the use of being a vision if you can't appear to someone now and again? It's not like we can impress each other. Keep me? Ha! No, not that. At best you might glimpse me again from a distance . . . but oooonly if you're not looking. Hope all you want, what the fuck do I care? Or slice your wrists. Whatever. It's all the same. It's all the same.

# Small Mercies
Heidi Decker

**Scene:** A small city park, outside an art museum

**Dramatic**
Dominick (45–60), a man searching for pieces of the big picture.

As Dominick wanders through the park, he ruminates on how quickly time passes while searching for scraps of paper that he believes are part of life's big picture.

DOMINICK: Days go by it seems really slowly, until you look up and see where you are. Where you're standing. It, it tears at me, this, every second, every second I'm awake and when I sleep it's all I dream about. Days go by they go by I try, I try to hold on, I reach out and grab two handfuls and hold on as long as I can . . . and then, I look, I look at my hands and I see that they're not mine. I don't recognize them, I must have picked up someone else's by mistake . . . so I let go to get a closer look at them and while I'm looking the day flies away. They are mine, after all. Only mine. My fingers are freezing. I'm one of those people whose fingers are always cold. When I touch people they shriek. And jump. I shriek when people touch me too, but for different reasons. I'm just always surprised. I think I just lost another day. I'm not sure, but it feels like it. I was walking, out, looking, and it fell out of my pocket, I'm sure of it now. Damn. *(In explanation.)* I tend to get distracted. I have to hold more tightly. I must get a better grip. I have to hold . . . hold . . . it. Hold it back, Hold it up. Hold it. Hold it. Hold everything. I hate having my hands so cold all the time . . . but I can't wear gloves. I can't breathe if I'm wearing gloves. I don't know why, I just can't. This wasn't always the way, I don't think. *I* wasn't, always. But I've found most of them now, the pieces. There's just a few more. . . So. I watch the ground, looking. That's what I do. Have been doing. Watching the ground, retracing my steps . . . I keep the others, the ones I've found so far, pinned inside my coat.

*(Opens coat briefly to show various scraps of paper and garbage pinned to the lining of his coat.)*

I'm nearly there, I'm pretty sure. They're not all fitted together yet . . . I don't think you can really do that until you have them all. You can't know what the picture will be with just parts. *(Pause.)* So how will I know when I have all of them? Yeah, well, *that's* the tricky part. But I'm *close,* I know it. I just have to stay focused. Just *(Coughs.)* just . . . until I get them. Then I can see . . . what . . . . . what it is. All put together. *(Pause, thoughtful.)* I wonder . . . if it'll be big.

# Sweet Butterfly on an Alligator's Lip
Richard Lay

**Scene:** A mansion in Charleston

**Dramatic**
  Buster (20s), black, emotionally delicate and anxious to please.

  Buster has been working as Lavinia's butler since they were both released from a mental hospital. Here, he shares a memory of their shared time in the clinic.

BUSTER: When we were in there. When we were in the CLINIC we didn't know the difference between crying and laughing, remember. We didn't know the difference between love, remorse, or despair. Remember when we sat doing a jigsaw puzzle and you asked me what my name was and I said: "I want to be what your called." And you said "I'm nothing honey." So I said "Why don't we call each other Nothing Honey." You just looked at me funny but I knew I'd made a connection. You said you had to sit next to the pay phone in case it rang for you. Just in case somebody cared enough to call you. I sat at your feet waiting for that phone to ring and you let me take your slippers off and rub your feet.
[LAVINIA: It didn't ring did it?]
BUSTER: For other people, who stepped over us . . . but it didn't matter. I had your feet and you had my hands and it seemed that we were very wealthy in that place.
[LAVINIA: They had some very nice flowers.]
BUSTER: They had state-of-the-art sprinklers. The grass was as green as Ireland. I never knew if the doctors and nurses cared. They never talked to us, did they. They just wrote things down. And they all had yellow pencils. Did you notice that . . . only yellow pencils.

# Sweet Butterfly on an Alligator's Lip

Richard Lay

**Scene:** A mansion in Charleston

**Dramatic**
   Pump (20s), an opportunist in love.

   Pump has fallen in love with Vanya, a young woman who claims to have been raped by Serbian soldiers. Pump and Vanya have made their way to Charleston where they drop in on Lavinia and Buster, who spent time with Pump in a mental hospital. Here, Pump tells Buster how he met Vanya, which is all a lie. In reality, Vanya is a New York–born con woman.

PUMP: Well, I'd kill myself for Vanya. I was over there as a relief worker and I found her lying on the steps of a church. Those bastards violated her and as they hurt her they ordered the street kids to ring the bells. I came into town with some Red Cross people and I thought she was dead. I kneeled over her and she opened her eyes. And in an instant, instead of me being just Pump, I became two people. She was part of me in that split second. So Buster, we're talking serious shit here . . . I'm not joking.
[BUSTER: When did all this happen?]
PUMP: Coupla months ago. She's here as a refugee. We've been at a military base. Her family are all fucked up or probably dead. All the NATO-UN dodos are running around doing whatever they do. All I know is I am in your house with Vanya and I'm looking at your ugly mug. Hey, buddy, got a beer. Don't worry about her. She drinks milk.

# Sweet Butterfly on an Alligator's Lip
Richard Lay

**Scene:** A mansion in Charleston

**Dramatic**
   Buster (20s), black, emotionally delicate and anxious to please.

   When Lavinia demands that Buster prove his devotion, he makes the following declaration of love.

BUSTER: I love you. I have told you I love you . . . I want to be with you . . . You don't hold my color against me . . . You treat me as an equal. You don't care that I can't read or tell the time. You don't care that I think white people—except you—are racist scum. You don't care that I have terrible body odor and bad breath. You often wonder what it would be like to make love to me and in your fantasies you wonder what I look like nude. You wouldn't care what your country club snobby friends would think if they thought we slept together. You would take me to their garden parties and flaunt me as your negro . . . You have no shame and that earns you my respect. If you choose me and I inherit the mansion and the money—I will spend your millions on establishing this house as a college for black kids from the ghetto . . . If you choose me I will teach you to love collard greens, Nat King Cole and old re-runs of Amos and Andy TV shows. Yes'M . . . I will be your loving husband Buster Tom, Uncle Tom, Cousin Tom and Tom Tom . . . I plight my troth and if you turn me down my heart will be leaden and I will start saving money to return to Africa—the land of my fathers—and will never darken your doorstep again. Lordy, lord.

# **Texas**
Judy Soo Hoo

**Scene:** A small, cramped trailer on the scene Texas Flats

**Dramatic**
>Danny (18–20), Asian American; a disturbed young man who witnessed the gruesome death of his parents.
>
>Danny and his brother, Duke, have tricked a college student, Steve, into moving into their isolated trailer with an offer of free housing. Here, Danny tells Steven of his failed relationship with a young Vietnamese girl he calls "Pooh Bear."

DANNY: I love Pooh Bear.
[DUKE: Danny's in his girly phase.]
[STEVEN: He's in love with Pooh Bear?]
DANNY: Hiep Li Ahn Tran, a.k.a. Pooh Bear. She's my Pooh Bear. She has hair as black as hell and a smile as kinked as the fiercest bombing run in Saigon. She wakes up scared as a fox in a foxhole with a pack of hounds chasing her. She wakes up with firebombs holed up in her head. She wakes up with the rattle-tat-tat of machine guns, of missiles bursting in midair, of raining shrapnel. She wakes up with shots shooting past her ear, blowing it off in little itty-bitty shreds. She wakes up war-spooked. But she's my Pooh Bear, my honey, my baby, a little spawn born in a hell called Vietnam.
[DUKE: She's spooky looking too.]
DANNY: All right. All right. She's a little spooky looking. It's on account of her face. Her left side of her face is fissured, cracked, creviced with burn scars from a nappy explosion of Napalm. But her right side of her face is lovely, creamy and smooth. Her left, burnt. Her right, beautiful. Burnt. Beautiful. Burnt. Beautiful.
>*(Danny illustrates by covering alternate sides of his face with the palms of his hands.)*

DANNY: The left side of her face will make your stomach turn over, turn black, turn away. But on the right side of her face, she's an angel, a honey, a sweet nectar of a peach.

[DUKE: They fooled around.]

DANNY: We fooled around. My Pooh Bear's stomach poofed up and poofed out.

[DUKE: Pooh Bear is going to have a bear cub.)

DANNY: When Pooh Bear's stomach poofed out, something snapped and broke, something fractured and fizzled, something happened to Pooh Bear.

[STEVEN: What? What?]

DANNY: Pooh Bear has scary dreams. She dreams scary dreams even when her eyes are open wide. In her waking dreams, things burn up, fire rolls on the ground, falls into cracks. She's running away from communists shooting at her back, from the killer firecracker weapons falling from the American planes high bombing. She sidesteps a minefield, swims across the South China Sea, survives a pirate attack. With the help of missionary men, she runs straight into the arms of Texas. She asks me, "What the hell am I doing in Texas?" (Pause.) We had such a short time together, then she snapped and then she's gone.

[STEVEN: What do you mean gone?]

DANNY: She's gone over. She's gone over the deep walls, the electric fence and the metal gate. She's gone in the dark cave, the marked corners, the belly of the beast. She's gone into the bughouse. My bear cub is in there, too, trapped. She's gone in and I have to get her out. I have to get her out and our bear cub too! But I don't want to go back. I don't want to go in.

# Threnody

David-Matthew Barnes

**Scene:** A one-room house in rural California, summer 1989

**Dramatic**
>Jake (20s), a guilt-ridden speed addict poised on the brink of oblivion.

>On the tail end of a three-day jag, Jake here muses about his lover, Dana, who has just confessed her unhappiness with their life in the country.

JAKE: You know what I was thinking about? How we met at that club . . . you were a city girl in a black skirt, sipping on a Sloe Gin Fizz . . . and then I asked you to dance . . . I gave you my number and it took you two days to call me . . . but you did. Then it was back and forth for us. Me going to the city. You coming out here. We just kept going . . . back and forth. Like marbles. I was supposed to get married when I met you. Monica still hates me. She came into the hardware store the other day and she just stared at me with these icy cold eyes, like she wanted to spit on me. Just like my old man. She looked at me, just the same. I just stood there, like an idiot. And I smiled at her. I was kinda hoping that she would have forgiven me by now. No such luck. She wishes that I was dead.

*(He snorts two lines.)*

Dana, I remember the first weekend that you and I spent together. I had to drive you to the bus depot. Right there, in front of God and everybody, I kissed you. I could feel your heart . . . ba-boom . . . ba-boom . . . like a heart attack. Then you looked at me. And I thought you were gonna cry, because you usually do. But I knew that you loved me. Nobody ever looked at me they way you did that day. Your eyes . . . they were so warm to me. I could tell you were sad, Dana. In fact, when I first saw you . . . I knew. I knew it was going to be this. Living together and making spaghetti. Getting wired and staying up for days. I wasn't gonna marry a rich girl named Monica. No way. I got me a Dana. She wants to write herself a best-seller. She wants to go to Paris someday because when she was a little girl, her grandmother sent her a postcard and she wanted to crawl inside of the picture. And she makes these crazy wishes on those glow-in-the-dark stars I put up on the ceiling above the bed. She sees herself up there. She is higher than high. She wants to be famous and take me with her on the ride, but she feels like she's got to hurry. She's scared I might get bored of it all and just say fuck it.

# Vernon Early
Horton Foote

**Scene:** Texas, 1950s

**Dramatic**
   Vernon Early (50s), a hard-working country doctor haunted by the loss of his adopted son.

   Following an exhausting all-night house call, Vernon here breakfasts with friends and shares memories both poignant and painful.

VERNON: You know what I was thinking about all the way drivin' over here? Teddy. Every once in awhile I think I'll just dig around and find out where he is and what's become of him.
[HARRY: Do you know his name now?]
VERNON: Oh, sure. Leroy.
[HARRY: Leroy?]
VERNON: Yes, Leroy Hayhurst.
[HARRY: How old would he be now?]
VERNON: Twenty-three. If I passed him on the street I doubt if I'd even recognize him. Of course, he wouldn't know me from Adam.
[HARRY: Teddy was the little boy Mildred and Vernon almost adopted.]
[REENIE: Oh, yes. I remember you're telling me. That was so sad.]
VERNON: I tell you that was a terrible day when the agency called just a month before the adoption became final and said the mother had changed her mind and wanted the boy back.
[REENIE: Why did she change her mind?]
VERNON: Well, she'd had the baby without her mother's knowing it, and then just before the legal time was up, her grandmother died and the girl got stricken by remorse during the wake and confessed to her mother what she had done and the mother went to the boy that got her pregnant and made him marry her

daughter and then they went to the agency and asked for the baby back and the agency called me, and said it was their legal right to do so, but I decided to take it to court and I spent a fortune let me tell you fighting for him in the courts. I finally went to the girl and her mother and offered her $50,000 if she would let us keep the baby. *(A pause.)* But no. No way. The day we gave him back it was like a funeral. Mildred cried for months. I never thought I would get over the hurt, but I did, of course, I did. That was almost the hardest thing I had to get over. Almost. *(He starts out again. He pauses.)* I guess maybe the worst was when Jack Henry died from lockjaw. I was his doctor. In those days we didn't automatically give tetanus shots when you broke your arm, and this boy was always falling and breaking something and getting well, mending so fast, and this fall was by a stable and he got an infection. *(A pause.)* And the Henry's have never let me forget the death of that boy. Never. When Steve Henry was trying to build a filling station across from our house, and Mildred was trying to stop him, he turned on her one day in the drugstore and said your husband killed one of my children and now you're trying to take bread away from the mouth of the other one. *(A pause.)* And things get back to you. That hurt. When I refused to fix Cassie's steps, that Preacher son of Jack Grayson's told someone that we'd learned nothing when God took the little boy from us, that all we thought of was the almighty dollar—that nothing else mattered. I sent a carpenter out to Cassie's and had the damn steps fixed but all the time that no-good son of Cassie's was telling everybody would listen—everybody—black or white how Cassie had worked for my mother for forty-five years for three dollars a week and how my mother had always promised to leave her money when she died to take care of Cassie; but left her nothing and that all I did, with all my money, was to let her stay rent-free in a leaking nigger shack that I couldn't get anybody to pay rent for. *(A pause.)* What he didn't tell was how we fed half the nigra's of Harrison from our kitchen, Cassie, her son and all their kind and the ones they didn't feed in the kitchen, they would take her food to give to their friends in the quarters. I was sitting in my breakfast room one noon and I saw that old nocount son of Cassie's coming out of Mama's kitchen totin' enough food to feed all of the quarters and I ran out of the house and I ordered him to take every bit of that food back. He did, too, by God. Anyway, once when Jack Grayson's Preacher son was here on a visit we invited him out to supper and he declined. I heard later he said he felt like telling me to give the money we would spend on his food to Cassie.

[HARRY: What was the name of Cassie's son? I forgot.]

VERNON: Solomon. I used to say to Mama get rid of him. Tell him to stay away from your kitchen. What good are you doin' him feeding him this way. Oh, I can't do that to Cassie's son she'd say. The truth was it had nothin' to do with Cassie, but Mama's brother, who she supported too, whenever he would get on one of his drunks and go wanderin' across the track to the quarters, she'd call Solomon day or night and he'd go find him for her and bring him home or else take him to his house until he slept off his drunk. *(A pause.)* Last night I went out to Miss Ethel Dennis's in the middle of the night because Velma was drunk again, and I'm the only one that can quiet her, and I thought, I am so tired, I will never make it out there, and when I left I was to have breakfast with Charles Johnson, but I was too tried to make it back to town and I pulled up by the side of the road and I went to sleep and the sun woke me up and I decided to come here and really sleep.

*(A pause.)* Do you realize Harry, Mildred and I are the only family now left living on that once quiet street of ours. All the other houses on the street have been abandoned.

[HARRY: I know and it was a lovely street too, beautiful old houses.]

VERNON: It has turned into an inferno now—an inferno of all-night food stands, filling stations, used car lots, the cotton and the oil trucks roaring by day and night, and the people—our friends, Harry, that once lived in the houses. Think of the terror that has pursued all of them. Even after they sold their houses and left. The Vaughns, the Taylors, the Johnsons, the Watts, the Gayles, the Gautiers. The most evil, vengeful fiend could not have imagined the horrors that have descended on our friends and their children and their children's children as if some evil spirit was determined to not only scatter the people living on that street but to pursue them vengefully, eternally.

# What Corbin Knew
Jeffrey Hatcher

**Scene:** A V.I.P. Hospitality suite, a skybox, high up in the entertainment complex of a large, second-tier American city

**Serio-comic**
Marshall (40s), well-fed and well-off, suffering from unrequited love.

Married Marshall has fallen in love with Thada, a student in his writing class. When she makes it clear that she will never have sex with him, he determines to kill himself. Here, he composes his last will and testament.

MARSHALL: This is the last will and testament of Marshall F. Allard. I, Marshall F. Allard, being of sound mind and body do hereby leave my cash, stocks, mutual funds, T-bills and moveable assets to my wife Margo, who says I have never grown up . . . with the exception of the following personal items: my "Man from UNCLE" lunch box I leave to my friend and partner Victor, honest, ethical Victor to whom I'm sorry for leaving our business in such a state of complete and utter ruin. My collection of James Bond action figures and the vintage four-inch model Aston Martin DB-4 I leave to my beloved son Trevor, who played with the car so much when he was in his crib that he broke the bulletproof screen and swallowed the little Korean guy sitting in the ejector seat next to 007. Last I leave my cherished . . . *(Chokes up.)* . . . my cherished, vintage red Mustang convertible to . . . Thada Pankoff. By the time you learn of this bequest, Thada, I will be gone from this world, but I want you to know that I told Margo we had an affair, a full passionate, sexual affair even though you told me time and again, over and over, to the point of nausea that although we could meet at the motel to read your writing and discuss it . . . ours could be only a platonic affair with kisses on the cheeks and hands held in friendly affection. I told Margo a lie that I wanted to believe and in the process hurt dozens, thousands, perhaps millions of people, if Margo is to be believed. Last. Last, I feel I should be honest with you, Thada. *(Beat.)* You are a very bad writer. I do not say these words to hurt you, but as I am dead now I feel I should be completely honest. Your writing stinks. Don't waste your life on it. Leave the profession and get a job in an Emory Board factory. I would never tell you this while I was alive, because I was still hoping you'd go to bed with me, but now that I am beyond this vale of tears I feel it's safe, knowing that however much I hurt you now, you won't be able to deny me the sexual congress I never had. Still . . .

*(The bottle of wine is now empty. Marshall sticks one leg over the balcony.)*

. . . it pains me more than I can say to know I shall never ever again set eyes on your lovely face ever, ever ag—

# Wild Man
Christopher Woods

**Scene:** Here and now

**Serio-comic**
Young Man (20–30), struggling to find himself in this confusing contemporary world.

Following stints in organizations ranging from A.A. to Sexually Confused Anonymous, this intrepid voyager has finally found himself in the men's movement . . . or has he?

*(A young man wears a furry loincloth and bells around his ankles. He wears war paint. He enters, chanting, dancing, generally whooping it up like an Indian. He carries a flag which is rolled up around the staff. He places the staff in a holder, then dances some more, chanting and beating a tom-tom.)*

YOUNG MAN: Okee! Okii! Okee! *(Repeat five or six times.) (To audience.)* I'm pretty contemporary. That's what everyone says. *Contemporary.* I like it. Even if I don't know what it means. So, when someone tells me, "God, you're contemporary," I just give my knowing smile.

*(Beats drum.)*

Okee! Okii! Okee! *(Repeats and dances.)*

It's not just about money. Sure, I have some. I'm not stupid. I own a condo. Twelve suits. An entry-level BMW. Membership to a gym. Invest in mutual funds. I own seven brands of cologne. I wear designer underwear. *(Looks at his loincloth and smiles.)* I have subscriptions to *Details* and *GQ*. It all feels good until I realize something. I don't know who I am. Not a clue. Sometimes it even bothers me. My old therapist, the one I don't see anymore, said I was asking too much from life. It doesn't matter *who* you are, he told me. Just keep on, that was his advice. I saw his point.

If I ever figured out who I was, he'd lose his patient. The longer I stayed in the dark, the better off *he* was. I don't talk about this stuff with my new therapist.

*(Beats drum.)*

Okee! Okii! Okee! *(Repeats while dancing.)*

I'm into self-realization, but I'm not there yet. I tried incense, even chewed it. Dropped acid. Sniffed liquid paper. Tried astral projection, but not enough to qualify for frequent flier miles. I've gone to tent revivals. I've kissed poisonous snakes. Lived for a few months on an ashram in Oregon, until I got worms. I've walked on hot coals, and blistered the shit out of my feet. Sure, I've abused myself. And abused most every drug there is. But at least it all led me to some good groups—A.A., N.A., C.A. Just last week, I joined S.C.A. (Sexually Confused Anonymous). Hey, didn't I tell you I'm a contemporary guy? But nothing solved my problem. *Who was I?* All I had to show for my efforts were a lot of new screwed-up friends I tried to avoid. *(Beat.)* Sound familiar?

*(Begins beating drum again.)*

So I joined the Men's Movement. Oh, I wasn't sure it would be right for me. Still, I know one thing about myself. I'm better off in a group. And hey, it's been fun. Where else would I get to wear war paint? I really like the Wild Man Weekends. We go camping. Sure, I'm afraid of ticks and Lyme disease, but it's worth the risk. Before, I was a soft male. But now, thanks in part to my drum *(Holds it high.)*, I FEEL LIKE A WARRIOR!

*(He unfurls the flag, which has a large, cartoonish penis inscribed on it. He dances and waves the flag.)*

Can you hold this for me? *(Hands the flag to an audience member.)* Thanks! Hold it high. Be proud!

*(Beats the drum, then continues.)*

Oh, I've sweated with the best of them. Run nude in the woods. Washed my mink jockstrap in mountain streams. Sang campfire songs about manhood. Hell, who needs women? Not me, at least for now. And there's another great advantage. I stay so busy, looking for my manhood *(Peers inside his loincloth.)*, I don't have time to worry about all the problems in the world! It's great!

*(He encourages the audience to join in.)*

All together now! Okee! Okii! Okee! *(Beat.)* I can't hear you. Let's try it again. Okee! Okii! Okee! Better, but you're not there yet.

*(He enters the audience to encourage them. Ad-libbing is fine.)*

Ready? OKEE! OKII! OKEE! *(Beat.)* I think you've got it!

*(Returns to center stage.)*

I've been in the Men's Movement for three months. Like I said, it's great. *(Slight pause.)* Well, maybe not that great. Matter of fact, it sucks. I've got to admit it. It's a crybaby movement. *(Looks forlorn, then brightly.)* But soon enough, something else will come along. It always does. And I'll be the first to sign up. I'm cutting edge. I'm contemporary. Hey, if you hear of anything, you'll let me know, won't you? *(Looks at an audience member.)* Hey, thanks! I knew *you* would.

*(Beats drum, begins dancing.)* Okee! Okii! Okee! *(Repeats while dancing.)*

*(Lights fade slowly to black.)*

**NOTE: These monologues are intended to be used for audition and class study; permission is not required to use the material for those purposes. However, if there is a paid performance of any of the monologues included in this book, please refer to the permissions acknowledgments below to locate the source who can grant permission for public performance.**

*The Adulterer* Copyright 1999 by Jussi Wahlgren Reprinted by Permission of the Author For International Performing Rights contact: Charles Aerts Theatre Productions International Valeriusplein 20 1075 BH Amsterdam Holland 20-6732285 Represented in the United States by: Frank Tobin 213-661-3720 Or Contact: Jussi Wahlgren Kukkaniitymtie 17 00900 Helsinki Finland

*Bad Buddhists* Copyright 1999 by Robert Vivian Reprinted by Permission of the Author Contact: Robert Vivian 4724 Davenport, #1 Omaha, NE 68132 (402) 553-7168

*Blue Food* "Blue Food" "Chocolate Kisses" "Honey" Copyright 1999 by Janice Fronczak Reprinted by Permission of the Author Contact: Janice Fronczak (314) 977-2994

*Blue Skies Forever* Copyright 1990 by Claire Braz-Valentine Reprinted by Permission of the Author Contact: Claire Braz-Valentine 4160 Jade Street #31 Capitola, CA 95010 cbrazvalen@aol.com

*Charlie & Flo* Copyright 1999 by Laurie Graff, All Rights Reserved Reprinted by Permission of the Author Contact: Laurie Graff 155 West 81st Street #1C New York, NY 10024

*Chicken Shit or Mengele's Mosquito* Copyright 2000 by Keith Kennedy Reprinted by Permission of the Author Contact: Keith Kennedy 55 St. Anne's Crescent Lewes, Sussex BNY 1SD UK

*The Connie Saxon Show* Copyright 1999 by Ethan Kanfer Reprinted by Permission of the Author Contact: kreplach99@aol.com

*Dueling Writers* Copyright 1999 by Mark Bellusci Reprinted by Permission of the Author Contact: Mark Bellusci 104 Hemlock Drive Stamford, CT 06902 (203) 363-0072

*Echoes From The Street* Copyright 1999 by Corey Tyler, All Rights Reserved Reprinted by Permission of the Author Contact: Jocelyn Beard Smith & Kraus kitowski@computer.net

*The Electric Hotdog Machine* Copyright 1999 by Le Wilhelm, All Rights Reserved Reprinted by Permission of the Author Contact: Cynthia Granville 162 Nesbit Weehawken, NJ 07087 (201) 601-2431

*Eve of Crimes: Memory Motel* Copyright 1999 by Bob Jude Ferrante Reprinted by Permission of the Author Contact: Bob Jude Ferrante 616 East 19th Street Brooklyn, NY 11230 (718) 421-6977

*The Feast of The Flying Cow…and Other Stories of War* Copyright 1999 by Jeni Mahoney, All Rights Reserved Reprinted by Permission of the Author Contact: Susan Schulman, A Literary Agency 454 West 44th Street New York, NY 10036 (212) 713-1633 schulman@aol.com

*Flat Tire* Copyright 1999 by David Fleisher Reprinted by Permission of the Author Contact: David Fleisher 4130 Tivoli Court #302 Lake Worth, FL 33467 dfleis1662@aol.com

*The Good Daughter* Copyright 1999 by Dolores Whiskeyman Reprinted by Permission of the Author Contact: Dolores Whiskeyman PO Box 10643 Arlington, VA 22201

*Hanging Lord Haw-Haw* Copyright 2000 by Jeffrey Hatcher Hanging Lord Haw-Haw by Jeffrey Hatcher was originally commissioned and produced by The Empty Space Theatre, Seattle, WA. Reprinted by Permission of the Author CAUTION: Professionals and amateurs are hereby warned that performance of Hanging Lord Haw Haw by Jeffrey Hatcher is subject to royalty. It is fully protected under the copyright laws of the United States of America, and of all countries covered by the International Copyright Union (including the Dominion of Canada and the rest of the British Commonwealth), and of all countries covered by the Pan-American Copyright Convention and the Universal Copyright Convention, the Berne Convention and of all countries with which the United States has reciprocal copyright relations. All rights, including professional, amateur/motion picture stage rights, recitation, lecturing, public reading, radio broadcasting, television, video or sound recording, all other forms of mechanical or electronic reproduction, such as CD-ROM, CD-1, information storage and retrieval systems and photocopying, and the rights of translation into foreign languages, are strictly reserved. Particular emphasis is laid upon the matter of readings, permission for which must be obtained from the author's agent in writing. Contact: Abrams Artist Agency 275 7th Avenue 26th Floor New York, NY 10001 Attention: Charmaine Ferenczi

*Heading West* Copyright 1999 by Philip Goulding Reprinted by Permission of the Author Contact: Eric Glass, Ltd. 28 Berkeley Square London W1X 6HD UK

*The Invention of Love* Copyright 1998 by Tom Stoppard CAUTION: Professionals and amateurs are hereby warned that performance of The Invention of Love by Tom Stoppard is subject to royalty. It is fully protected under the copyright laws of the United States of America, and of all countries covered by the International Copyright Union (including the Dominion of Canada and the rest of the British Commonwealth), and of all countries covered by the Pan-American Copyright Convention and the Universal Copyright Convention, the Berne Convention and of all countries with which the United States has reciprocal copyright relations. All rights, including professional, amateur/motion picture stage rights, recitation, lecturing, public reading, radio broadcasting, television, video or sound recording, all other forms of mechanical or electronic reproduction, such as CD-ROM, CD-1, information storage and retrieval systems and photocopying, and the rights of translation into foreign languages, are strictly reserved. Particular emphasis is laid upon the matter of readings, permission for which must be obtained from the author's agent in writing. First class professional applications for permission to perform them, etc. must be made in advance, before rehearsals begin, to Peters, Fraser and Dunlop Ltd. 503/4 The Chambers, Chelsea Harbor, London SW10 0XF, and stock and amateur applications for permission to perform them, etc., must be made in advance, before rehearsals begin, to Samuel French, Inc. 45 West 25th Street, New York, NY 10010 Reprinted by permission of Grove Press Contact: Grove Press 841 Broadway 4th Floor New York, NY 10003

*The Judas Kiss* Copyright 1998 by David Hare Reprinted by Permission of Grove Press CAUTION: Professionals and amateurs are hereby warned that performance of The Judas Kiss by David Hare is subject to royalty. It is fully protected under the copyright laws of the United States of America, and of all countries covered by the International Copyright Union (including the Dominion of Canada and the rest of the British Commonwealth), and of all countries covered by the Pan-American Copyright Convention and the Universal Copyright Convention, the Berne Convention and of all countries with which the United States has reciprocal copyright relations. All rights, including professional, amateur/motion picture stage rights, recitation, lecturing, public reading, radio broadcasting, television, video or sound recording, all other forms of mechanical or electronic reproduction, such as CD-ROM, CD-1, information storage and retrieval systems and photocopying, and the rights of translation into foreign languages, are strictly reserved. For Performance Rights Contact: International Creative Management 40 West 57th Street New York, NY 10019 Attention: Sam Cohn All other inquiries contact: Grove Press 841 Broadway 4th Floor New York, NY 10003

*Just Taking Up Space* Copyright 1998 by Nancy Gall-Clayton Originally Produced by Horse Cave Theatre, Warren Hammack, Producing Director Reprinted by Permission of the Author Contact: Nancy Gall-Clayton 1375 South Second Street Louisville, KY 40208-2303 nancyjea@lou-ky.win.net

*The Killer and the Comic* Copyright 1999 by Rooster Mitchell Reprinted by Permission of the Author Contact: International Creative Management 8942 Wilshire Blvd. Beverly Hills, CA 90211 (310) 550-4000 (310) 550-4100 – Fax Attention: Barbara Mandel, Agent

*Listening to Insomnia* Copyright 1999 by Amy Beth Arkawy Reprinted by Permission of the Author Contact: Amy Beth Arkawy 12 Elm Hill Drive Rye Brook, NY 10573

*Louis Slotin Sonata* Copyright 1999 by Paul Mullin Reprinted by Permission of the Author Contact: Fifi Oscard Associates 24 West 40th Street 17th Floor New York, NY 10018 Attn. Carolyn French, author's agent

*The Martyrdom of Washington Booth* Copyright 1999 by Jeni Mahoney, All Rights Reserved Reprinted by Permission of the Author Contact: Susan Schulman, A Literary Agency 454 West 44th Street New York, NY 10036 (212) 713-1633 Schulman@aol.com

*The Most Fabulous Story Ever Told* Copyright 1999 by Paul Rudnick Reprinted by Permission of Helen Merrill, Ltd. on behalf of the Author CAUTION: Professionals and amateurs are hereby warned that The Most Fabulous Story Ever Told by Paul Rudnick is subject to royalty. It is fully protected under the copyright laws of the United States of America, and of all countries covered by the International Copyright Union (including the Dominion of Canada and the rest of the British Commonwealth), and of all countries covered by the Pan-American Copyright Convention and the Universal Copyright Convention, the Berne Convention and of all countries with which the United States has reciprocal copyright relations. All rights, including professional, amateur/motion picture stage rights, recitation, lecturing, public reading, radio broadcasting, television, video or sound recording, all other forms of mechanical or electronic reproduction, such as CD-ROM, CD-1, information storage and retrieval systems and photocopying, and the rights of translation into foreign languages, are strictly reserved. Particular emphasis is laid upon the matter of readings, permission for which must be obtained from the author's agent in writing. The stage performance rights in The Most Fabulous Story Ever Told (other than first class rights) are controlled exclusively by Dramatists Play Service, 440 Park Avenue South, New York, NY 10016. No professional or non-professional performance of the Play (excluding first class professional performances) may be given without obtaining in advance the written permission of Dramatists Play Service, and paying the requisite fee. Inquiries concerning all other rights should be addressed to: Helen Merrill, Ltd. 295 Lafayette Street Suite 915 New York, NY 10012-2700

*New York Actor* Copyright 1999 by John Guare Reprinted by Permission of Dramatists Play Service Contact: Dramatists Play Service 440 Park Avenue South New York, NY 10016

*No One Talks to the Mailman* Copyright 1999 by Christopher Wall Reprinted by Permission of the Author Contact: christopher.wall.92 @alum.dartmouth.org

*Perfect World* Copyright 1999 by Linda Stockham Reprinted by Permission of the Author Contact: Linda Stockham 5500 University Parkway San Bernadino, CA 92407-2397 1stockha@csusb.edu

*The Power of Love* Copyright 1999 by Sebastian Michael Reprinted by Permission of The Rod Hall Agency, Ltd. Contact: Clare Barker, Author's Agent The Rod Hall Agency, Ltd 7 Goodge Place London W1D 1FL UK 171-637-0706 171-637-0807 – fax rod.hall@dial.pipex.com

*A Question of Mercy* Copyright 1998 by David Rabe CAUTION: Professionals and amateurs are hereby warned that A Question of Mercy by David Rabe is subject to royalty. It is fully protected under the copyright laws of the United States of America, and of all countries covered by the International Copyright Union (including the Dominion of Canada and the rest of the British Commonwealth), and of all countries covered by the Pan-American Copyright Convention and the Universal Copyright Convention, the Berne Convention and of all countries with which the United States has reciprocal copyright relations. All rights, including professional, amateur/motion picture stage rights, recitation, lecturing, public reading, radio broadcasting, television, video or sound recording, all other forms of mechanical or electronic reproduction, such as CD-ROM, CD-1, information storage and retrieval systems and photocopying, and the rights of translation into foreign languages, are strictly reserved. Reprinted by permission of Grove Press Contact: Grove Press 841 Broadway 4th Floor New York, NY 10003

*Rim of the Wheel* Copyright 1998, 2000 by Daphne R. Hull Reprinted by Permission of the Author Contact: Daphne R. Hull 230 West Lanvale Baltimore, MD 21217 ink@ix.net-com.com

*Shoes* Copyright 1999 by Sky Vogel Reprinted by Permission of the Author Contact: Sky Vogel 30 Evergreen Avenue Clifton Park, NY 12065

*The Significant Betrayal* Copyright 1999 by Le Wilhelm, All Rights Reserved Reprinted by Permission of the Author Contact: Cynthia Granville 162 Nesbit Weehawken, NJ 07087 (201) 601-2431 CreekRead@aol.com

*Sinatragate* Copyright 1999 by Bob Jude Ferrante Reprinted by Permission of the Author Contact: Bob Jude Ferrante 616 East 19th Street Brooklyn, NY 11230 (718) 421-6977

*Small Mercies* Copyright 1999 by Heidi Decker Reprinted by Permission of the Author Contact: Heidi Decker 200 Vuemont Place #C106 Renton, WA 98056 HEDecker@aol.com

*Sweet Butterfly on an Alligator's Lip* Copyright 1999 by Richard Lay Reprinted by Permission of the Author Contact: Richard Lay 205 West 15th Street 2M New York, NY 10011

*Texas* Copyright 1999 by Judy Soo Hoo Reprinted by Permission of the Author Contact: Judy Soo Hoo 11550 Nebraska Avenue #110 Los Angeles, CA 90025 (310) 478-2208

*Threnody* Copyright 2000 by David-Matthew Barnes Reprinted by Permission of the Author Contact: The Dorothy Nickle Performing Arts Company 2221 West Giddings Street Chicago, IL 60625 Attention: Harriet Russell, Literary Department

*Vernon Early* Copyright 1999 by Horton Foote Reprinted by Permission of Dramatists Play Service CAUTION: Professionals and amateurs are hereby warned that Vernon Early by Horton Foote is subject to royalty. It is fully protected under the copyright laws of the United States of America, and of all countries covered by the International Copyright Union (including the Dominion of Canada and the rest of the British Commonwealth), and of all countries covered by the Pan-American Copyright Convention and the Universal Copyright Convention, the Berne Convention and of all countries with which the United States has reciprocal copyright relations. All rights, including professional, amateur/motion picture stage rights, recitation, lecturing, public reading, radio broadcasting, television, video or sound recording, all other forms of mechanical or electronic reproduction, such as CD-ROM, CD-1, information storage and retrieval systems and photocopying, and the rights of translation into foreign languages, are strictly reserved. Contact: The Gersh Agency 130 West 42nd Street New York, NY 10036 Attention: Peter Hagan, Agent

*What Corbin Knew* Copyright 2000 by Jeffrey Hatcher What Corbin Knew by Jeffrey Hatcher was originally commissioned and produced by Madison Repertory Theatre Reprinted by Permission of the Author CAUTION: Professionals and amateurs are hereby warned that performance of What Corbin Knew by Jeffrey Hatcher is subject to royalty. It is fully protected under the copyright laws of the United States of America, and of all countries covered by the International Copyright Union (including the Dominion of Canada and the rest of the British Commonwealth), and of all countries covered by the Pan-American Copyright Convention and the Universal Copyright Convention, the Berne Convention and of all countries with which the United States has reciprocal copyright relations. All rights, including professional, amateur/motion picture stage rights, recitation, lecturing, public reading, radio broadcasting, television, video or sound recording, all other forms of mechanical or electronic reproduction, such as CD-ROM, CD-1, information storage and retrieval systems and photocopying, and the rights of translation into foreign languages, are strictly reserved. Particular emphasis is laid upon the matter of readings, permission for which must be obtained from the author's agent in writing. Contact: Abrams Artist Agency 275 7th Avenue 26th Floor New York, NY 10001 Attention: Charmaine Ferenczi

*Wild Man* Copyright 1999 by Christopher Woods Reprinted by Permission of the Author Contact: Christopher Woods 2229 Mimosa #1 Houston, TX 77019